Praise for previous editions:

"*The State of the World Atlas* is something else – an occasion of wit and an act of subversion...These are the bad dreams of the modern world, given color and shape and submitted to a grid that can be grasped instantaneously."
New York Times

"Unique and uniquely beautiful...a discerning eye for data and a flair for the most sophisticated techniques of stylized graphic design; the atlas succeeds in displaying the geopolitical subtleties of global affairs in a series of dazzling color plates...tells us more about the world today than a dozen statistical abstracts or scholarly tomes."
Los Angeles Times

"Coupled with an unusual non-distorting map projection and a series of brilliant cartographic devices, this gives a positively dazzling set of maps. It deserves to be widely used."
New Society

"A super book that will not only sit on your shelf begging to be used, but will also be a good read. To call this book an atlas is like calling Calvados, applejack – it may be roughly accurate but it conveys nothing of the richness and flavour of the thing. Its inventive brilliance deserves enormous rewards."
New Scientist

"A striking new approach to cartography...no-one wishing to keep a grip on the reality of the world should be without these books."
International Herald Tribune

"Outspoken cataloguing of global oppressions and inequities, painstakingly sourced."
Independent on Sunday

"Packed with fascinating facts and figures on everything from the international drugs industry to climate change."
Evening Standard

"A political reference book which manages to translate hard, boring statistics into often shocking visual statements... required reading."
NME

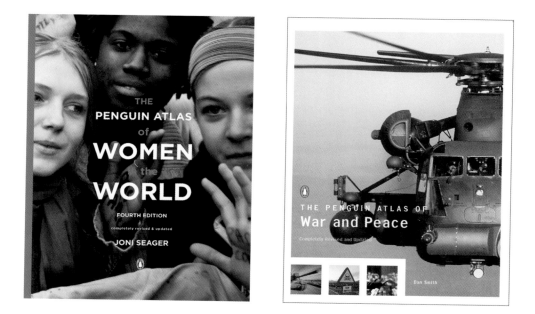

THE PENGUIN
STATE OF THE WORLD
ATLAS

Completely Revised and Updated
Eighth Edition

Dan Smith

PENGUIN BOOKS

PENGUIN BOOKS
Published by the Penguin Group
Penguin Group (USA) Inc., 375 Hudson Street, New York, New York 10014, U.S.A.
Penguin Group (Canada), 90 Eglinton Avenue East, Suite 700, Toronto,
Ontario, Canada M4P 2Y3 (a division of Pearson Penguin Canada Inc.)
Penguin Books Ltd, 80 Strand, London WC2R 0RL, England
Penguin Ireland, 25 St Stephen's Green, Dublin 2, Ireland
(a division of Penguin Books Ltd)
Penguin Group (Australia), 250 Camberwell Road, Camberwell, Victoria 3124,
Australia (a division of Pearson Australia Group Pty Ltd)
Penguin Books India Pvt Ltd, 11 Community Centre, Panchsheel Park,
New Delhi – 110 017, India
Penguin Group (NZ), 67 Apollo Drive, Rosedale, North Shore 0632,
New Zealand (a division of Pearson New Zealand Ltd)
Penguin Books (South Africa) (Pty) Ltd, 24 Sturdee Avenue, Rosebank,
Johannesburg 2196, South Africa

Penguin Books Ltd, Registered Offices: 80 Strand, London WC2R 0RL, England

This eighth edition first published in Penguin Books 2008

3 5 7 9 10 8 6 4

Copyright © Myriad Editions Limited 2008

Penguin paperback ISBN is 978-0-14-311452-9

Produced for the Penguin Group by
Myriad Editions
59 Lansdowne Place
Brighton, BN3 1FL, UK
www.MyriadEditions.com

Edited and coordinated by Jannet King and Candida Lacey
Designed by Isabelle Lewis and Corinne Pearlman
Maps and graphics by Isabelle Lewis

Printed on paper produced from sustainable sources.
Printed and bound in Hong Kong through Lion Production
under the supervision of Bob Cassels, The Hanway Press, London

Contents

Part One: Who We Are

Part Two: Wealth and Power

Part Three: War and Peace

Part Four: Rights and Respect

Part Five: Health of the People

Part Six: Health of the Planet

Part Seven: Vital Statistics

Author

Dan Smith is Secretary General of the London-based
international peacebuilding organization International Alert and
former Director of the International Peace Research Institute, Oslo (PRIO).
He is the author of *The State of the Middle East*, as well as successive editions of
The State of the World Atlas and *The Atlas of War and Peace*.
In 2002 he was awarded an OBE.

Credits

Myriad is pleased to have been able to select all of the Part Title images as well as many of the smaller photographs from **Panos Pictures**, an independent photo agency representing photojournalists worldwide. Their photographers document issues and geographical areas that are under-reported, misrepresented or ignored. In a media climate dominated by celebrity and lifestyle Panos aims to provide fresh perspectives on the world. Half of the profits from the agency are given to the Panos Institute to further its work on issues around media and communications, globalization, HIV/AIDS and environment and conflict.

In addition to the Panos photographers named below, we are grateful to the following for permission to reproduce their photographs on the following pages: 16 Mark Henley / Panos Pictures; 20 World Bank / Curt Carnemark; 24 Jennifer Trenchard / iStockphoto; 25 William Holtby / Circa Religion Photo Library; 26 World Bank / Trevor Sansom; 28 World Bank / Ray Witlin; 30 Los Angeles: Simon Horton / Panos Pictures; Cairo, London, Mumbai and New York: Candida Lacey; Mexico City: Milan Klusacek / iStockphoto; São Paulo: AM29 / iStockphoto; Paris: J B Russell / Panos Pictures; Lagos: George Osodi / Panos Pictures; Istanbul: George Georgiou / Panos Pictures; Karachi: Giacomo Pirozzi / Panos Pictures; Tokyo: Wikimedia Commons / Chris 73; 31 Jakarta: Martin Adler / Panos Pictures; Shanghai: Manfred Leiter; 32 iStockphoto / Glenn Frank; 34 Ian Teh / Panos Pictures; 36 World Bank / Yosef Hadar; 40 World Bank / Anatoliy Rakhimbayev; 42 iStockphoto / Joseph Luoman; 46 iStockphoto / Pamela Moore; 49 iStockphoto / Cliff Parnell; 50 iStockphoto / Jan Will; 52 top: iStockphoto / Izabela Habur; bottom: iStockphoto / Juergen Sack; 54 UNICEF India / Ami Vitale; 56 Iva Zimova / Panos Pictures; 60 George Georgiou / Panos Pictures; 61 Tomas van Houtryve / Panos Pictures; 63–64 Elio Colavolpe / Panos Pictures; 68 Lutfallah Daher / Associated Press; 72 top: Ash Sweeting / Panos Pictures; bottom: Jenny Matthews / Panos Pictures; 73 Andrew Testa / Panos Pictures; 76 Philippe Lissac / Panos Pictures; 79 Panos Pictures / Jacob Silberberg; 81 Erik Millstone; 86 Eric Gevaert / iStockphoto; 89 top: Sadashivan; bottom: American Cancer Society Inc; 91 UK Parliament; 93 iStockphoto / Ericsphotography; 94 Teun Voeten / Panos Pictures; 96 left: George Gerster / Panos Picture; right: World Food Programme / Sabrina Quezada; 100 World Health Organization / Harry Anenden; 102 American Cancer Society Inc / Chris Hamilton; 106 Alvaro Leiva / Panos Pictures; 108 Panamanian golden frog: www.messiah.edu; 111 iStockphoto / kshishtof; 113 top: Algalita Marine Research Foundation www.algalita.org; bottom: Greenpeace / Natalie Behring; 117 A Ishokon / UNEP / Still Pictures; 122 Dieter Telemans / Panos Pictures.

We would also like to thank Peter H Dana, The Geographer's Craft Project, University of Colorado at Boulder for use of map projections (p.14), ODT maps / www.odtmaps.com for permission to adapt the population cartogram (pp.18–19), the International Institute for Strategic Studies and Taylor & Francis for use of data from *The Military Balance 2008* (pp.64–69, 130–37) and the Institute for Economics and Peace for use of their 2008 Global Peace Index / www.visionofhumanity.org (pp.74–75). We have made every effort to obtain permission for the use of copyright material. If there are any omissions, we apologise and shall be pleased to make appropriate acknowledgement in any future edition.

Introduction

The world faces some formidable challenges. If it were possible to make progress on five key ones – poverty, power, war, health and the natural environment – there would be grounds for real optimism about the prospects of moving towards a world of greater fairness and justice. The catalogue of problems is grim but they are all, in principle, open to solution.

Poverty

Today, more people are being lifted out of poverty than ever before, but a long-term problem of economic development persists. Not only are the gains of development unevenly distributed, but they have come at the price of eroding long-established social and cultural ties that have been of great benefit to people, and the old ways are not always replaced with equally viable new ones.

At the same time, despite progress on poverty reduction, inequality persists and the gap between the richest and the poorest in the world shows little sign of narrowing. The issue is not only injustice but also whether billions can be lifted out of poverty if the condition of people in the world remains so deeply marked by inequality. For, without a redistribution of existing wealth the poor can only get a little wealthier – unless substantially more wealth is generated. But can economic growth and development continue at today's pace, and for how long? Natural resources are not infinite, nor is the world's capacity to absorb waste, and keeping up "business as usual" means more emissions of greenhouse gases, thus accelerating global warming. If the world's population keeps growing, and without redistributing wealth, it seems as if there must be limits to poverty reduction.

And there is a further sustainability issue. The world's population is aging. On current projections, while the total population will increase by over 35 percent by 2050, the economically active part of the population will hardly grow at all. What quality of life will the working population enjoy in view of the extra burden they will have to carry?

In other words, pursuing the current model of economic development offers us a view of the future that is unsustainable for society and the natural environment.

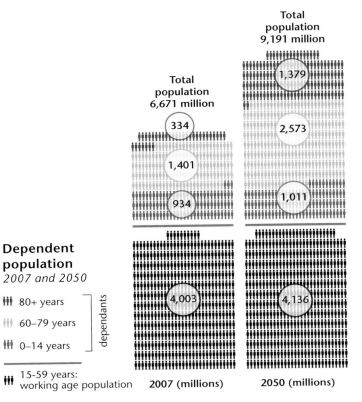

Dependent population
2007 and 2050

- ⫯⫯⫯ 80+ years
- ⫯⫯⫯ 60–79 years
- ⫯⫯⫯ 0–14 years
  } dependants

⫯⫯⫯ 15-59 years: working age population

Total population 6,671 million

334
1,401
934
4,003

2007 (millions)

Total population 9,191 million

1,379
2,573
1,011
4,136

2050 (millions)

Power, participation and exclusion

The 19th and 20th centuries, despite wars and colonialism, experienced significant expansion of political rights and freedoms. The process frequently hit obstacles, when there seemed a risk of progress being blocked or even reversed. Yet, despite sham democracies in some countries and local reverses, there is more real freedom of political choice worldwide and more legal recognition of a fuller ranger of human rights than ever.

But are we now hitting a new period of obstacles and risks of reversals, in some countries at least? Some of the opportunities for extending democracy that arose in the former Soviet bloc countries after the end of the Cold War appear to have been spurned. And the real threat of terrorism in the first decade of this century has been used by some western governments to justify restricting rights and freedoms. What makes this more worrying is that in some countries, perhaps because long familiarity with political freedoms has dulled awareness of their fundamental importance, there has been a marked decline in public confidence in politicians and in the political process, and therefore in political participation.

War and peace

Conditions of injustice feed violent conflict. Yet the surprisingly good news in today's world is that there are fewer wars now than 20 years ago, and that they are, in general, less lethal. The number of peace agreements to end civil wars in the years since the end of the Cold War in 1989–91 exceeds the number reached during the previous 200 years. The proportion of peace agreements that fail within the first five to 10 years also appears to be dropping. Horrors persist, and some conflicts have been suppressed rather than settled, but the overall trend is positive.

There is, however, a new question to which we should also attend. Is the nature of violent conflict changing? Wars between states have become relatively rare. The predominant kind of warfare since the end of World War II, and especially in the last two decades, has been *within* states rather than *between* them. Relatively

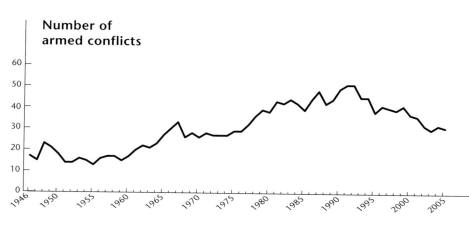

Number of armed conflicts

recently, the phenomenon of non-state wars has become visible – wars in which neither party is a state. It has also long been clear that in civil wars the business of fighting shades into criminal activity such as smuggling diamonds or cocaine, robbing banks, kidnapping or running protection rackets, to raise funds for the cause. And in some cases, the idea of a cause has rather slipped into the background. In conflicts of the future, in the mega-cities, for example, political and criminal conflict may be pretty much indistinguishable.

The health of the people ...

It is not only the risk of social conflict that stands out when we look at marginalization and poverty. It is the basic question of health. At least 1 billion people worldwide lack access to clean water, 1.5 billion do not have enough water, and 3 billion do not have sanitation. These are conditions in which health suffers and disease flourishes. On top of this, the HIV/AIDS pandemic has devastated parts of Africa. The ill-health of the people lead to further doubts about the viability of current models of economic development.

In the rich world, health problems also persist. The largest single preventable cause of death is tobacco smoking. Obesity is an increasing problem and is associated with numerous diseases. The result will be to put increasing pressure on health services that also have to cope with an increasing proportion of the population that is getting to an age when reasonable health is maintained only by increasing medical attention.

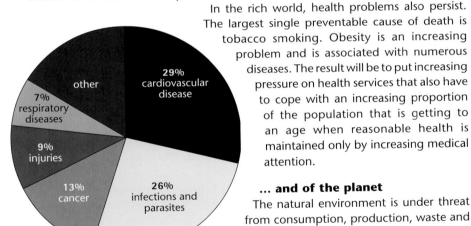

Major causes of death
as percentage of all deaths
2008

(pie chart segments:)
29% cardiovascular disease
26% infections and parasites
13% cancer
9% injuries
7% respiratory diseases
other

... and of the planet

The natural environment is under threat from consumption, production, waste and greenhouse gases. The global food crisis that emerged in the first half of 2008, as this atlas was being prepared, is the product of many factors, including short-term price speculation, but it is partly driven by changes in climate. These changes are broadly consistent with the predictions of climate models exploring the consequences of global warming. If we do not start to learn how to treat the natural environment with more care, there will be parts of the world where human habitats will become less habitable, with consequences including conflicts, migration and further instability in neighbouring areas.

Problems with solutions

Solutions to these issues are not easy, but nor are they impossible. Progress on democracy and human rights can resume if we use the rights and freedoms that we have. There are fewer wars now than only a few years ago. Progress has been made on

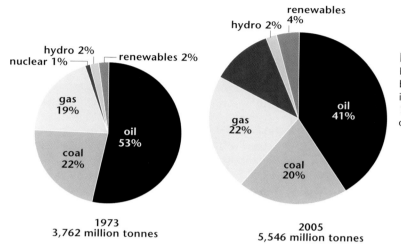

Energy production
Percentage of energy produced
by each type of fuel
in OECD countries
1973 & 2005
oil equivalent

renewables 4%
hydro 2%
oil 41%
gas 22%
coal 20%

2005
5,546 million tonnes

hydro 2%
nuclear 1%
renewables 2%
gas 19%
oil 53%
coal 22%

1973
3,762 million tonnes

poverty reduction and there can be more if political parties and leaders start to recognize that inequality is ultimately as much of the problem for those on top of the pile as for those at the bottom. While climate change throws down an enormous challenge, measures to reduce greenhouse gas emissions are technically feasible, but they come at a price and so far in most countries politicians have not found a way both to let the price be paid and to get re-elected. While the benefits of reducing emissions feed through the natural system, it will also be necessary for the countries that are vulnerable to climate change consequences in the short term to adapt to face the problems. Most of them are poor, and large-scale international assistance will be needed. It will be expensive but affordable for the rich world that caused the problem. And if the basic problems of power, peace, poverty and climate change are resolved, the scale of some of the issues of human health will be reduced to manageable proportions. In short, these are serious problems but solutions are, in principle, available.

Knowing the world
No single government can take on these big challenges and solve them. They will be addressed by agreement among governments or not at all. Elected governments need to be pressed to act by public opinion. Even non-democratic governments can often be influenced by international opinion. To generate that pressure, we need to know the issues and understand them.

But watch out for the trap of over-reliance on facts. Take the example of climate change. To insist on getting the facts about climate change before deciding whether and how to act means waiting, and, if the climate projections and scientists' estimates are right, that means waiting until it is too late. This was the posture of the US government under George W. Bush. If we accept the clear majority scientific view about the risks of inactivity on climate change, then we have to learn how to act before all the facts are in, and adjust as we go along if necessary. We have to act even when knowledge and understanding are always provisional. In a deep sense, we need to make it up as we go along.

That said, while knowing and understanding the facts may not be enough, it is essential. Projections and estimates about many issues, not just the consequences of climate change, build on known facts about the past and present to construct a picture of the future. But the knowledge and understanding that must be called on to help shape a world of justice and fairness are not only scientific. Local communities, for example, often know much more about the conditions in which they live than experts and scientists do. We need to learn how to combine abstract knowledge with the wisdom derived from experience and tradition, enriching both, in order to find peaceful solutions to difficult conflicts, to include marginalized groups in key decisions, to understand what is happening in the natural environment.

There is, in fact, a global storehouse of knowledge and understanding that is every bit as impressive as the problems and challenges we face. The issue is how to deploy it. Knowledge is very often the possession of a relatively small group of experts. Yet decisions on these issues affect everybody and should not be the purview only of a small group, however well qualified. They have extremely broad implications and need to be shaped not by narrow expertise but with reference to the bigger picture.

Statistics ...

This series of *State of the World* atlases, which was initiated in 1982, and of which this is the eighth edition, has endeavoured to present the provisional facts about key world issues in a way that is reliable, digestible for the non-expert, and oriented towards revealing the larger picture. These books do not offer – and do not claim to offer – the only definitive worldview. They simply offer to help you see the broad outlines, the context for deeper knowledge on specific issues.

Running through the series' treatment of world issues over the years, one common thread has been the difficulty of knowing the world. The series – and likewise the related atlases on the state of women, war and peace, the Middle East, China, the environment, health, water, food, endangered species and others – grew from a choice to offer broad, global perspectives, drawing on world-level statistics, expressed visually as far as possible, with the main visual technique being world maps.

That choice has been fruitful but it does raise a couple of tricky issues. The closer one gets to statistics and the more one works with them, the more the words of 19th-century British prime minister Benjamin Disraeli are borne out. There are three kinds of lies, he said: lies, damned lies, and statistics. Statistics and the yearbooks in which they are published are indispensable, tricky, less reliable than they seem, and often consist of a quicksand of mutable assumptions, varying minutely and without notice from case to case and year to year. The world as seen through the statistical lens is often blurred, and individual countries can sometimes look quite strange.

... and maps

Choosing an atlas format means facing up to the problem of maps. Because the world is virtually round, it cannot be accurately depicted on a flat, rectangular piece of paper. Peel an orange and flatten out the skin and the problem is immediately understandable. Choices and compromises must accordingly be made – choices, essentially, about how to be inaccurate. These choices are packaged into the *projection* of the world that is utilized in drawing the map. The most widely seen world maps use projections that retain the shapes of the continents and islands, and therefore wildly distort their size. The most famous of these projections is the one developed by the 16th-century Flemish cartographer, Gerardus Mercator. Using that projection, the sizes of regions far from the equator are exaggerated. Thus, Europe looks bigger than it is, while China and India look smaller. The most notorious distortion of area in Mercator is that Africa looks smaller than Greenland but is actually 14 times bigger. Mercator's choice of projection was determined in part by his wish, as the sub-title of the original atlas put it, to produce an aid for navigators. Navigation was at the forefront of Europe's advance into the world between the 15th and the 18th centuries. Accurate cartography was the scientific precondition for sailing to far-flung destinations for trade and conquest.

There have been numerous attempts over succeeding centuries to correct the illustrative weakness in the Mercator projection. The best-known today is the one proposed in 1973 by Arno Peters, drawing on work in the 19th century by a Scottish clergyman, James Gall. The Peters, or Gall-Peters, projection is more accurate on the size of different regions but distorts the world's appearance in other ways. There are geographers who believe the depiction of the world on rectangular pieces of paper should be stopped.

This atlas uses the 1913 Winkel Tripel; the "Tripel" refers to the three elements of area, direction and distance, between which Oswald Winkel compromised. The distortions are not eliminated but – check Greenland against Africa – they are minimized, and are mostly visible at the poles. This projection's curved lines of latitude and longitude make it useless for navigators, but the result is fairer and has become reasonably familiar, especially since it was adopted by the US National Geographic Society in 1998. Familiarity with approximate size and location of countries makes possible one of this atlas's ways of presenting information – the cartogram, which re-sizes countries to correspond to their relative scale when compared by size of population, for example, or number of armed forces.

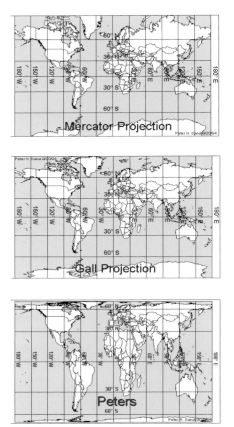

Acknowledgements

The atlas is the product of a team. Jannet King was responsible for most of the basic data research and has made a major editorial input. Isabelle Lewis kept thinking up innovative ways of graphically and cartographically presenting the information and, together with Corinne Pearlman, provided the creative oversight that gives the book its distinctive feel. Karina Kristiansen provided some life-saving research assistance late in the day. Candida Lacey ran and coordinated the Myriad team and me, and was, as with earlier editions and other atlases, a joy to work with. I thank them all unreservedly.

Dan Smith
London, June 2008

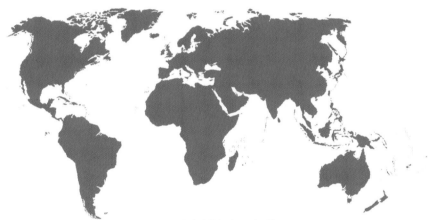

Myriad's world map based on the Winkel Tripel projection

Cartogram style

As countries get richer, the population grows more slowly. The world's population doubled in the second half of the 20th century, passing 6 billion at the start of the 21st. The rate of growth has slowed, especially in the two most populous countries – China and India – but on current trends the total will exceed 9 billion by 2050, with Africa and parts of the Middle East growing fastest.

Population growth
1820–2050 projected

1820 1 billion
1930 2 billion
1960 3 billion
1974 4 billion
1988 5 billion
2000 6 billion

2050 9 billion

MONGOLIA

CHINA
1,306m

NORTH KOREA
23m

SOUTH KOREA
49m

JAPAN
127m

KYRGYZSTAN

KAZAKHSTAN
15m

AZERBAIJAN

TAJIKISTAN

NEPAL
28m

BHUTAN

TAIWAN
23m

ORGIA

ARMENIA

UZBEKISTAN
27m

VIETNAM
84m

KEY

TURKMENISTAN

AFGHANISTAN
30m

LAOS

IRAN
68m

PAKISTAN
162m

INDIA
1,080m

BURMA
43m

IRAQ
26m

THAILAND
65m

PHILIPPINES
88m

KUWAIT

SAUDI ARABIA
26m

UNITED ARAB EMIRATES

OMAN

CAMBODIA
14m

YEMEN
21m

Every

1.25

**seconds
a baby
is born in
India**

BANGLADESH
144m

MALAYSIA
24m

PIA

SOMALIA

SINGAPORE

NYA

DA

QUE

MAURITIUS

MADAGASCAR
18m

SWAZILAND

SOTHO

SRI LANKA
20m

INDONESIA
242m

EAST TIMOR

PAPUA NEW GUINEA

AUSTRALIA
20m

NEW ZEALAND

People in the world
2006

☐ = 1 million

Annual percentage change

3.0% or more

2.0% — 2.9%

1.0% — 1.9%

0.1% — 0.9%

-0.1% — -1.1%

no data

Population map: © 2005, www.odtmaps.com

19

UK 79

USA 78

Japan 82

Mexico 75

China 72

Russia 66

India 64

World average life expectancy:

68 years

Haiti 53

CANADA

USA

Nigeria 47

BERMUDA

BAHAMAS

CUBA

DOMINICAN REP.

JAMAICA   HAITI

PUERTO RICO

MEXICO

BELIZE

GUATEMALA   HONDURAS

EL SALVADOR   NICARAGUA

COSTA RICA

PANAMA

VIRGIN IS. (US)

ST KITTS & NEVIS

ANTIGUA & BARBUDA

DOMINICA

GRENADA

N. ANTILLES

ST LUCIA

BARBADOS

ST VINCENT & GRENADINES

TRINIDAD & TOBAGO

VENEZUELA

COLOMBIA

GUYANA

SURINAME

ECUADOR

PERU

BRAZIL

BOLIVIA

CHILE   PARAGUAY

ARGENTINA

URUGUAY

Botswana 35

ICELAND

NORWAY   SWEDE

UK   DENMARK   LI

IRELAND   NETH.   RUSS

GERMANY   PO

BEL.   CZ.

LUX.   REP.

FRANCE   SWITZ.   AUS.

SL

CRO.   B.

MONT.·

PORTUGAL   SPAIN   ITALY

TUNISIA

MOROCCO   MAL

ALGERIA   LIB

CAPE VERDE

MAURITANIA   MALI   NIGER

SENEGAL

GAMBIA   BURKINA FASO

GUINEA-BISSAU   GUINEA   CÔTE D'IVOIRE   GHANA   TOGO   BENIN   NIGERIA

SIERRA LEONE   CEN AFR REP.

LIBERIA   CAMEROON

EQUATORIAL GUINEA   GABON

SAO TOME & PRINCIPE   CONGO

ANG

NAMIB

BOTSW

Three main factors influence average life expectancy: nutrition, water supplies and health services. Accordingly, wealth and longevity are closely related. Richer countries have a longer average life expectancy than poorer countries, and both in affluent and impoverished countries, the rich live longer on average. When rich countries are compared with each other, differences in life expectancy often reflect differences in society, in diet and in how health care is provided.

The average lifespan of people living in 30 countries in Sub-Saharan African is less than 50 years – the same as in the USA in 1900.

Expectations
Average number of years of life of a baby born in 2005

Life Expectancy

Russia
Life expectancy of men is only 59 years – 13 years lower than that of women.

Life expectancy
at birth
2005 or latest available data

- 35.0 – 49.0 years
- 50.0 – 69.9 years
- 70.0 – 79.9 years
- 80 years or more
- no data

Changing expectancy
1990–2005 or latest available data

↓ decrease of 7 or more years

↑ increase of 7 or more years

Health and wealth
Comparison of national wealth per capita and life expectancy
1980 & 2005

- low-income countries
- middle-income countries
- high-income countries

1980	2005	1980	2005	1980	2005
53 yrs	59 yrs	65 yrs	70 yrs	74 yrs	79 yrs
$603	$2,463	$1,735	$7,212	$9,643	$32,840

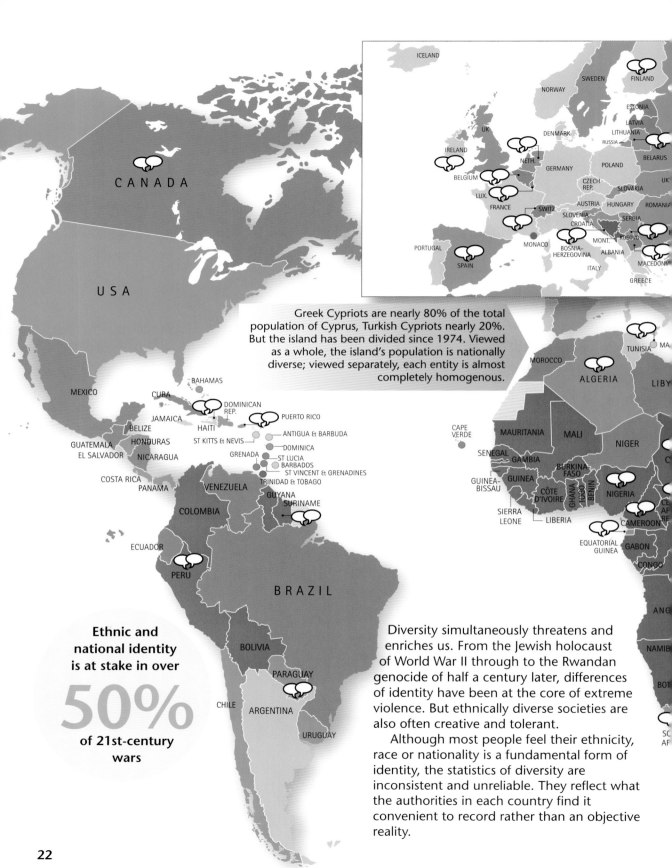

Greek Cypriots are nearly 80% of the total population of Cyprus, Turkish Cypriots nearly 20%. But the island has been divided since 1974. Viewed as a whole, the island's population is nationally diverse; viewed separately, each entity is almost completely homogenous.

Ethnic and national identity is at stake in over

50%

of 21st-century wars

Diversity simultaneously threatens and enriches us. From the Jewish holocaust of World War II through to the Rwandan genocide of half a century later, differences of identity have been at the core of extreme violence. But ethnically diverse societies are also often creative and tolerant.

Although most people feel their ethnicity, race or nationality is a fundamental form of identity, the statistics of diversity are inconsistent and unreliable. They reflect what the authorities in each country find it convenient to record rather than an objective reality.

Ethnicity and Diversity

RUSSIA

KAZAKHSTAN

MONGOLIA

NORTH
KOREA

JAPAN

SOUTH
KOREA

UZBEKISTAN

KYRGYZSTAN

GEORGIA

ARMENIA

AZERBAIJAN

TURKMENISTAN

TAJIKISTAN

CYPRUS

TURKEY

SYRIA

LEB.

JORDAN

IRAQ

KUWAIT

AFGHANISTAN

CHINA

TAIWAN

IRAN

PAKISTAN

NEPAL

BHUTAN

PALESTINE
AUTHORITY

ISRAEL

BAHRAIN

QATAR

UAE

EGYPT

SAUDI
ARABIA

OMAN

INDIA

BANGLADESH

BURMA

LAOS

THAILAND

VIETNAM

PHILIPPINES

YEMEN

ERITREA

DJIBOUTI

SUDAN

ETHIOPIA

SOMALIA

UGANDA

KENYA

RWANDA

BURUNDI

TANZANIA

SEYCHELLES

COMOROS

MALAWI

ZAMBIA

ZIMBABWE

MADAGASCAR

MAURITIUS

MOZAMBIQUE

SWAZILAND

LESOTHO

SRI LANKA

MALDIVES

SINGAPORE

MALAYSIA

BRUNEI

INDONESIA

AUSTRALIA

NEW
ZEALAND

Micronesia inset
MICRONESIA,
FED. STATES OF

MARSHALL ISLANDS

NAURU

KIRIBATI

SOLOMON
ISLANDS

TUVALU

VANUATU

FIJI

SAMOA

NEW
CALEDONIA

FRENCH
POLYNESIA

Indonesia
The government
identifies over
300 ethnic groups,
speaking over
700 languages.

Ethnic, national
and racial diversity
Minority group(s) as a proportion
of the population
2007 or latest census

under 10%

10% – 29%

30% – 49%

50% or more:
no single ethnic, national or
racial group forms more than half
of the population

data unavailable or inadequate

Language of government

 more than one
official language

Schools and Schisms
Most popular religion by group and sub-group

Buddhism
- Mahayana —— Chinese
- Tibetan
- Japanese
- Theravada

Christianity
- Catholicism — Protestantism
  - Lutheranism
  - Anglicanism
  - Calvinism
- Orthodox
- Christian Independents

Islam
- Sunni —— Hanafi
  - Hanbali
  - Maliki
  - Shafi
- Shi'a —— Ithna'ashaariyya
  - Zaydis
- Ibadiyyah

other religions
- Hinduism
- Judaism
- Chinese indigenous religion
- other indigenous beliefs
- atheism

Christians in the USA
Percentage by denominations
2006

- Independents 78.8 million
- Catholics 64.6 million
- Protestants 61 million

The world's largest religions are Christianity (about 2 billion believers) and Islam (just over 1 billion).

Religious belief has a strong influence on how people think and act and what they expect from life. Faith is a matter of individual conscience and for much of the world's people it is a source of stability and comfort. But religion's deep influence also makes it a profound marker of identity, so religious differences often align with the deepest cultural differences and social divisions. Where religious leaders cannot or will not restrain how those differences are expressed, heated and uncontrollable conflicts can explode. Some of the most brutal violence in the world's history – and still today – is inflicted in the name of religion. And differences within religions – between Sunni and Shi'a Muslims, for example, or between Protestant and Catholic Christians – are often as intense as differences between them.

Christianity is the world's largest religion with more than 2.1 billion adherents, and more than 33,000 denominations.

Religious Beliefs

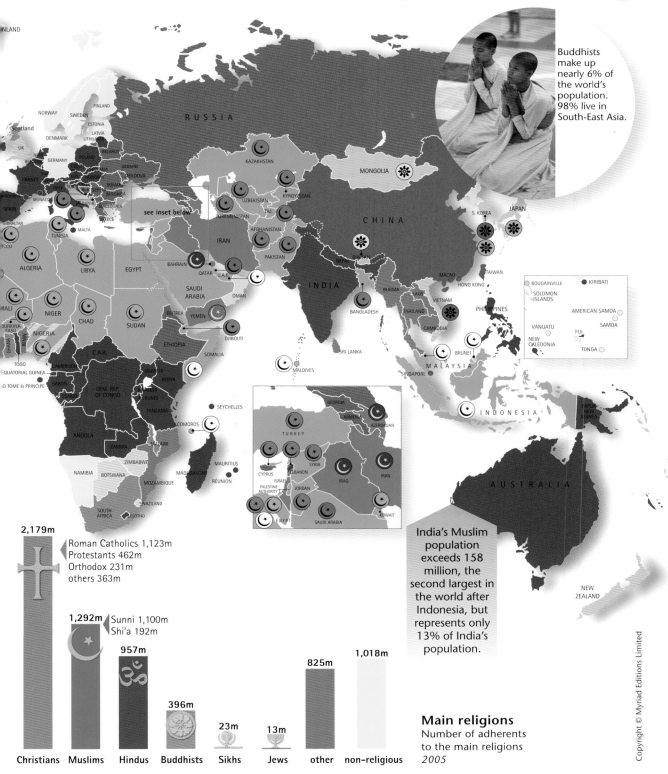

Buddhists make up nearly 6% of the world's population. 98% live in South-East Asia.

see inset below

India's Muslim population exceeds 158 million, the second largest in the world after Indonesia, but represents only 13% of India's population.

2,179m
Roman Catholics 1,123m
Protestants 462m
Orthodox 231m
others 363m

1,292m
Sunni 1,100m
Shi'a 192m

957m

396m

23m

13m

825m

1,018m

Christians | Muslims | Hindus | Buddhists | Sikhs | Jews | other | non-religious

Main religions
Number of adherents to the main religions
2005

57%
of children
not in school
are girls

There are
8 girls or fewer
for every
10 boys starting
school in
Afghanistan,
Central African
Republic, Chad,
Niger, Pakistan
and Yemen.

Primary education
Percentage of children
of the correct age
enrolled in primary school
2005 or latest available data

Secondary education
Percentage of children
of the correct age
enrolled in secondary school
2005 or latest available data

fewer than 10%

10% – 29%

30% – 49%

50% – 69%

Sub-Saharan Africa
There are only
8 girls in
secondary school
for every
10 boys.

Education

Sub-Saharan Africa
There are only 6 girls in tertiary education for every 10 boys.

Tertiary education
Percentage of young people enrolled in tertiary college
2005 or latest available data

- 70% – 90%
- 90% or more
- no data

Adult literacy
Literate adults as percentage of adult population
2005

Literacy is simultaneously a functional need for modern societies, a basic tool for individual advancement, and a rich benefit in everybody's personal life. As modern trade and industry have spread, so have general literacy levels. In most countries, discrimination at school and at home means that more women than men are illiterate and girls still lag behind boys in worldwide school enrolment statistics.

64% of illiterate adults are women

Bangladesh and India
Literacy percentage up 13 points since mid-1990s.

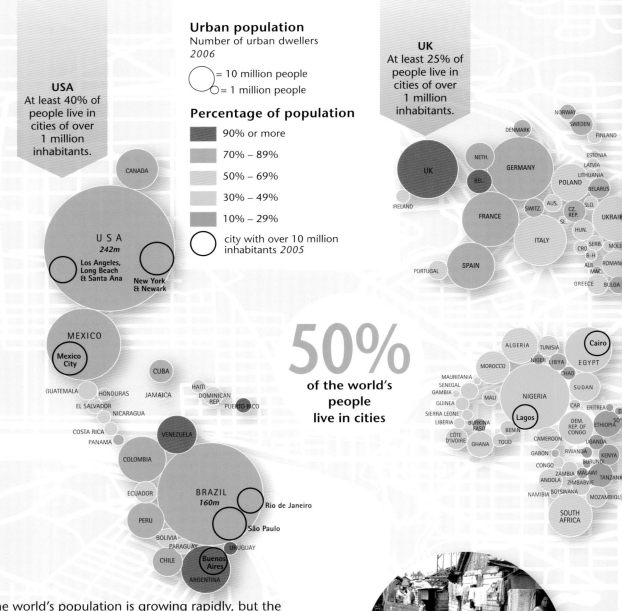

Urban population
Number of urban dwellers
2006

◯ = 10 million people
○ = 1 million people

Percentage of population

- 90% or more
- 70% – 89%
- 50% – 69%
- 30% – 49%
- 10% – 29%
- ◯ city with over 10 million inhabitants *2005*

USA
At least 40% of people live in cities of over 1 million inhabitants.

CANADA

U S A
242m

Los Angeles, Long Beach & Santa Ana

New York & Newark

MEXICO

Mexico City

CUBA

GUATEMALA
HONDURAS
EL SALVADOR
NICARAGUA
JAMAICA
HAITI
DOMINICAN REP.
PUERTO RICO

COSTA RICA
PANAMA

VENEZUELA

COLOMBIA

ECUADOR

BRAZIL
160m

Rio de Janeiro

São Paulo

PERU

BOLIVIA
PARAGUAY
URUGUAY

CHILE

Buenos Aires

ARGENTINA

50%
of the world's people live in cities

UK
At least 25% of people live in cities of over 1 million inhabitants.

NORWAY
SWEDEN
FINLAND

DENMARK

UK
NETH.
GERMANY
ESTONIA
LATVIA
LITHUANIA
BEL.
POLAND
BELARUS

IRELAND

FRANCE
SWITZ.
AUS.
CZ. REP.
SLO.
UKRAIN
SL.
HUN.

ITALY

CRO.
SERB.
B-H
MOLI

PORTUGAL
SPAIN
ALB.
MAC.
ROMAN

GREECE
BULGA

ALGERIA
TUNISIA
Cairo
EGYPT

MOROCCO
NIGER
LIBYA

MAURITANIA
SENEGAL
GAMBIA
GUINEA
SIERRA LEONE
LIBERIA
MALI
CHAD
SUDAN

NIGERIA
CAR
ERITREA
D

BURKINA FASO
BENIN
Lagos
DEM. REP. OF CONGO
ETHIOPIA
SO

CÔTE D'IVOIRE
GHANA
TOGO
CAMEROON
UGANDA

GABON
RWANDA
KENYA
BURUNDI

CONGO

ZAMBIA
MALAWI
ANGOLA
ZIMBABWE
TANZAN

NAMIBIA
BOTSWANA
MOZAMBIQU

SOUTH AFRICA

The world's population is growing rapidly, but the urban population is growing even faster. The proportion of people living in cities is on the way from an estimated 40 percent in 1980 to 60 percent in 2020, and 70 percent in 2030.

New urbanization is largely concentrated in the developing countries. Most major cities in Europe are static or declining in size, partly because improved transport and communications are reducing the economic benefits of concentrating large numbers of people in a few places. In developing countries, however, the big cities remain magnets for people seeking livelihoods when they can no longer sustain themselves in the countryside.

Many cities are ringed by houses built by the urban poor, leading to tensions between the authorities and desperate people with nowhere else to go.

Urbanization

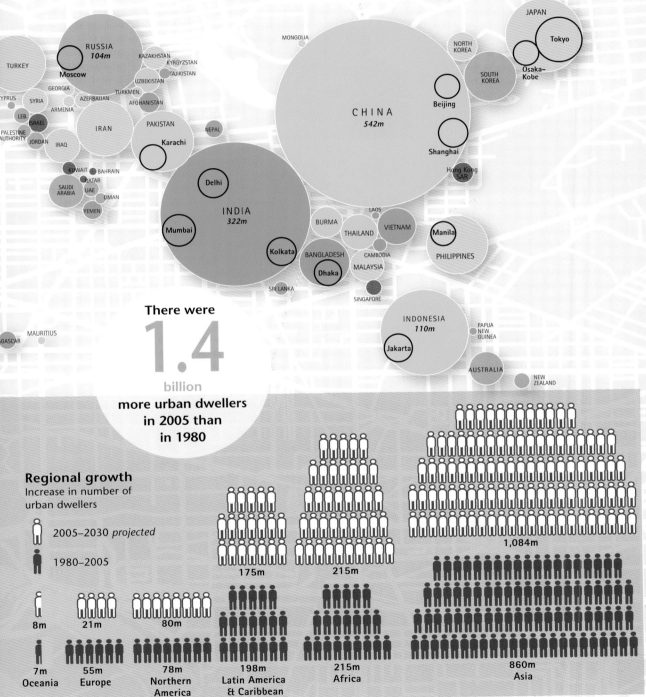

MONGOLIA

TURKEY

RUSSIA
104m
Moscow

KAZAKHSTAN

KYRGYZSTAN

TAJIKISTAN

UZBEKISTAN

TURKMEN.

AFGHANISTAN

AZERBAIJAN

GEORGIA

ARMENIA

CYPRUS

SYRIA

LEB.

ISRAEL

PALESTINE
AUTHORITY

JORDAN

IRAQ

IRAN

PAKISTAN

Karachi

NEPAL

KUWAIT

BAHRAIN

QATAR

SAUDI
ARABIA

UAE

OMAN

YEMEN

Delhi

INDIA
322m

Mumbai

Kolkata

BURMA

THAILAND

LAOS

VIETNAM

CAMBODIA

BANGLADESH

Dhaka

MALAYSIA

SRI LANKA

SINGAPORE

CHINA
542m

Beijing

Shanghai

NORTH
KOREA

SOUTH
KOREA

Hong Kong
SAR

JAPAN

Tokyo

Osaka–
Kobe

Manila

PHILIPPINES

MADAGASCAR

MAURITIUS

INDONESIA
110m

Jakarta

PAPUA
NEW
GUINEA

AUSTRALIA

NEW
ZEALAND

There were

1.4

billion

more urban dwellers in 2005 than in 1980

Regional growth
Increase in number of
urban dwellers

2005–2030 *projected*

1980–2005

8m

21m

80m

7m
Oceania

55m
Europe

78m
Northern
America

198m
Latin America
& Caribbean

175m

215m

215m
Africa

1,084m

860m
Asia

City wealth
Comparative rank of selected cities
2008 or latest available data

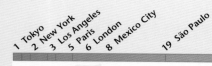

50% of residents are Latinos • 30% are Anglophone • 10% of Asian descent • 40% were born outside the USA • 20% live in poverty.

London, UK
Population **8m**
Area (sq km) **1,623**
Density (pop/sq km) **5,100**

30% of London residents are non-white • 95% of people moving to London since 1995 were born outside the UK.

Paris is the most visited city in the world – with 30 million annual visitors. Few visit its suburbs – except Disneyland and Parc Asterix • 20% of population of Greater Paris were born outside France.

Los Angeles
Population **12m**
Area (sq km) **4,320**
Density (pop/sq km) **2,750**

New York City, USA
Population **18m**
Area (sq km) **8,683**
Density (pop/sq km) **2,050**

48% of New Yorkers speak a language other than English at home.

70% of new jobs in Mexico City are in the "informal" sector (unregulated, unprotected by law) • its metro system is the world's cheapest and the fourth most used (4.5 million people a day).

Paris, France
Population **10m**
Area (sq km) **2,723**
Density (pop/sq km) **3,550**

Annual population growth of 5% equals 74 new residents per hour • Over 50% of Nigeria's industry is located in Lagos's suburbs.

Mexico City, Mexico
Population **17m**
Area (sq km) **2,072**
Density (pop/sq km) **8,400**

São Paulo is the largest Japanese city outside Japan; the largest Lebanese city outside Lebanon; the largest Spanish city outside Spain • 66% of population is under 20 years old.

São Paulo, Brazil
Population **18m**
Area (sq km) **1,968**
Density (pop/sq km) **9,000**

City income
US$ per capita
in selected cities
2008 or latest available data

Lagos, Nigeria
Population **13m**
Area (sq km) **738**
Density (pop/sq km) **18,150**

$62,900

$56,500

$53,300

$46,000

$36,000

$18,500

$14,800

New York | London | Los Angeles | Paris | Tokyo | Mexico City | Istanbul

Diagram of Cities
Diversity of Cities

Worldwide 3 billion people live in cities; 1 billion in urban slums. In Sub-Saharan Africa, over 70% of city-dwellers live in slums; in South and Central Asia, nearly 60%.

Istanbul has 19 new residents per hour • 50% of residents estimated to live in *gecekondus*, illegal constructions "built overnight" • over half of Turkey's international trade passes through Istanbul.

Istanbul, Turkey
Population 9m–12m
Area (sq km) 1,166
Density (pop/sq km)
7,700

99% of Tokyo's population is Japanese by birth • 40% of the city is built on landfill.

Tokyo, Japan
Population **33m**
Area (sq km) **6,993**
Density
(pop/sq km)
4,750

49% of Karachi's population are Urdu speakers, 19% Sindhi, 11% Punjabi, 9% Pashtun and 4% Balochi; the remaining 8% speak at least 14 other languages • Karachi's annual population growth of 5% equals 57 new residents per hour.

Karachi, Pakistan
Population **10m**
Area (sq km) **518**
Density (pop/sq km)
18,900

99% of Shanghai's residents were born and raised in China • 29 new residents added per hour • Shanghai had 1 skyscraper in 1988 and 300 less than 20 years later.

Shanghai, China
Population **10m**
Area (sq km) **746**
Density (pop/sq km)
13,400

60% of Cairo's inhabitants live in unlicensed housing • air pollution kills 10,000-25,000 each year.

Mumbai, India
Population **14m**
Area (sq km) **484**
Density (pop/sq km)
30,000

Over 50% of Jakarta's buildings are temporary or semi-permanent • 25% of Jakartans have daily access to clean water • only 2% use public transport

Cairo, Egypt
Population 12m–18m
Area (sq km) **1,295**
Density (pop/sq km)
9,400

50% of Mumbai's population has no sanitation • with 1% of India's population, Mumbai pays 40% of national tax revenues.

Jakarta, Indonesia
Population **14m**
Area (sq km) **1,360**
Density (pop/sq km)
10,500

$13,900	$12,500	$10,500	$8,200	$7,000	$5,500	$2,300
Shanghai	São Paulo	Mumbai	Cairo	Jakarta	Karachi	Lagos

The US economy relies heavily on the cheap labour provided by migrant workers – both legal and illegal.

GREENLAND

ICELAND

NORWAY

CANADA

UK
IRELAND
DENMARK
NETH.
GERMANY
BEL.
LIECHT.
LUX.
SWITZ.
FRANCE

USA

PORTUGAL SPAIN

ITALY

BERMUDA

TUNISIA

MEXICO

MOROCCO

ALGERIA

CAYMAN IS.
CUBA
BAHAMAS
DOMINICAN
REP.
PUERTO RICO
JAMAICA
HAITI
VIRGIN IS. (UK)
ANGUILA
ANTIGUA & BARBUDA
St KITTS & NEVIS
GUADELOUPE
BELIZE
MONTSERRAT
DOMINICA
HONDURAS
GRENADA
MARTINIQUE
St LUCIA
GUATEMALA
ARUBA
BARBADOS
EL SALVADOR
N. ANTILLES
St VINCENT & GRENADINES
NICARAGUA
TRINIDAD & TOBAGO
COSTA RICA
VENEZUELA
PANAMA
GUYANA
COLOMBIA
SURINAME
FRENCH GUIANA

WESTERN
SAHARA

CAPE
VERDE

MAURITANIA

MALI

NIGER

SENEGAL

GAMBIA
GUINEA-
BISSAU
GUINEA
BURKINA
FASO
NIGERIA
SIERRA LEONE
GHANA
TOGO
BENIN
LIBERIA
CÔTE
D'IVOIRE
CAMEROON
EQUATORIAL
GUINEA
SAO TOME
& PRINCIPE
GABON
CONG

ECUADOR

BRAZIL

PERU

Despite increasing global movement only

3%

of the world's people are living in a different country from where they were born

Trying to leave poverty behind and find good jobs and prosperity in a new place, many migrants take terrible risks on the journey and find a cold welcome if they survive and arrive. Although wealthier countries need immigrant workers, they do not usually treat them well. Newcomers are accused of stealing jobs even as their work contributes to economic growth. If these problem can be overcome, there is much evidence – not least from the US experience – that economies flourish and cultures benefit from the diversity that immigration brings.

BOLIVIA

CHILE
PARAGUAY

ARGENTINA

URUGUAY

38 million

Migrants
Largest populations
of migrants
2005

👤 500,000 people

12 million

10 million

USA

Russia

Germany

Global Movement

Gulf States
These countries rely heavily on migrant workers, in particular those from Pakistan, to work in their oil and construction industries.

Living abroad
People born outside country, excluding refugees, as percentage of population *2005*

50.0% or more	1.0% – 4.9%
25.0% – 49.9%	fewer than 1.0%
10.0% – 24.9%	
5.0% – 9.9%	

Immigration policy
to lower immigration

RUSSIA

KAZAKHSTAN

MONGOLIA

MOLDOVA

GEORGIA ARMENIA AZER. UZBEKISTAN KYRGYZSTAN

TURKEY TURKMENISTAN TAJIKISTAN

'PRUS SYRIA LEB. AFGHANISTAN

ISRAEL IRAQ IRAN

PALESTINE AUTHORITY JORDAN KUWAIT PAKISTAN

BAHRAIN QATAR

EGYPT SAUDI ARABIA UAE

OMAN

SUDAN ERITREA YEMEN

DJIBOUTI

ETHIOPIA

UGANDA SOMALIA

KENYA

RWANDA

BURUNDI

TANZANIA

COMOROS

SEYCHELLES

MALAWI

MADAGASCAR

MAURITIUS

RÉUNION

MOZAMBIQUE

SWAZILAND

LESOTHO

CHINA

NORTH KOREA

SOUTH KOREA

JAPAN

NEPAL BHUTAN

Hong Kong SAR

Macao SAR

INDIA BANGLADESH

BURMA LAOS

THAILAND VIETNAM

CAMBODIA

PHILIPPINES

SRI LANKA

MALDIVES

BRUNEI

MALAYSIA

SINGAPORE

INDONESIA

EAST TIMOR

PAPUA NEW GUINEA

GUAM NORTHERN MARIANA IS.

MICRONESIA, FED. STATES OF MARSHALL ISLANDS

NAURU KIRIBATI

SOLOMON ISLANDS TUVALU

AMERICAN SAMOA

SAMOA

VANUATU COOK ISLANDS

NEW CALEDONIA FIJI

TONGA NIUE

FRENCH POLYNESIA

PALAU

AUSTRALIA

NEW ZEALAND

2.6 million
people migrated from poorer to richer countries in 2005

6.8 million	6.5 million	6.4 million	6.1 million	5.7 million	5.4 million
Ukraine	France	Saudi Arabia	Canada	India	UK

The graffiti on the wall testifies to the power of the local Commando Vermelho (Red Command) drug cartel over the inhabitants of Cantagalo, a favela on the hillside above the wealthy resort of Ipanema, Rio de Janeiro, Brazil.

Country wealth

Gross National Income
(GNI) per capita
2006 or latest available data
PPP$

A PPP (Purchasing Power Parity) dollar
can buy the same in each economy as $1
does in the USA.

- $20,000 or more
- $10,000 – $19,999
- $5,000 – $9,999
- $1,000 – $4,999
- less than $1,000
- no data

Inflation

⬆ consumer price index
increased by 100% or more
2000–05

Gross National
Income (GNI) has
become the most
common way of
measuring a country's
wealth. It combines the
value of goods – the things
people make, grow or extract
from the ground – with the
value of services. It does not
distinguish between the other
merits of the goods or services
(such as whether they are
environmentally sound, socially
destructive, morally acceptable).
And it only offers a measure of
wealth – not an indication of how
it is used.

Many
economies,
and the
survival of
many people
living in them,
rely heavily on
money sent
home by citizens
working abroad,
many of whom
are themselves
living in
poverty.

Sending money home

Workers' remittances
as percentage of GDP
of receiving country
2006
selected countries

36% Tajikistan

22% Lebanon

CANADA

USA

MEXICO

GUATEMALA
EL SALVADOR
BELIZE
HONDURAS
NICARAGUA
COSTA RICA
PANAMA
JAMAICA
HAITI
DOMINICAN
REP.
ST KITTS & NEVIS
GRENADA
ANTIGUA & BARBUDA
DOMINICA
ST LUCIA
ST VINCENT & GRENADINES
TRINIDAD & TOBAGO

COLOMBIA
VENEZUELA
GUYANA
SURINAME
ECUADOR
PERU
BRAZIL
BOLIVIA
PARAGUAY
CHILE
ARGENTINA
URUGUAY

ICELAND
NORWAY
SWEDEN
UK
DENMARK
IRELAND
NETH
GERMANY
BEL
LUX
FRANCE
SWITZ
AUS.
ITALY
ANDORRA
MONACO
CRO.
PORTUGAL
SPAIN
POL
CZ
REP
LITH
RUSSI

TUNISIA
MALTA
MOROCCO
ALGERIA

CAPE
VERDE
MAURITANIA
MALI
NIGER
SENEGAL
GAMBIA
GUINEA-
BISSAU
GUINEA
SIERRA LEONE
CÔTE
D'IVOIRE
BURKINA
FASO
GHANA
TOGO
BENIN
NIGERIA
CAMEROON
EQUATORIAL
GUINEA
GABON
CONGO
CEN
AFR
REP.
NAMIBIA
BOTSWANA
ANGO

National Income

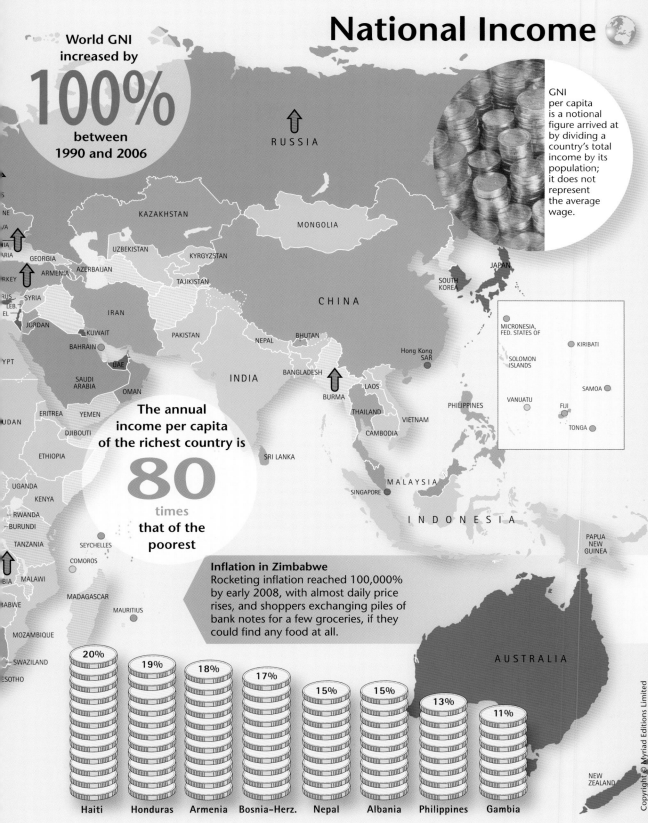

World GNI increased by

100%

between 1990 and 2006

GNI per capita is a notional figure arrived at by dividing a country's total income by its population; it does not represent the average wage.

RUSSIA

KAZAKHSTAN

MONGOLIA

UZBEKISTAN

KYRGYZSTAN

GEORGIA

ARMENIA

AZERBAIJAN

TAJIKISTAN

SYRIA

JORDAN

IRAN

CHINA

JAPAN

SOUTH KOREA

KUWAIT

BAHRAIN

UAE

SAUDI ARABIA

OMAN

PAKISTAN

NEPAL

BHUTAN

INDIA

BANGLADESH

Hong Kong SAR

BURMA

LAOS

THAILAND

VIETNAM

CAMBODIA

PHILIPPINES

ERITREA

YEMEN

DJIBOUTI

ETHIOPIA

SRI LANKA

MICRONESIA, FED. STATES OF

KIRIBATI

SOLOMON ISLANDS

VANUATU

FIJI

SAMOA

TONGA

UGANDA

KENYA

RWANDA

BURUNDI

TANZANIA

SEYCHELLES

COMOROS

MALAWI

MADAGASCAR

MAURITIUS

MOZAMBIQUE

SWAZILAND

LESOTHO

MALAYSIA

SINGAPORE

INDONESIA

PAPUA NEW GUINEA

The annual income per capita of the richest country is

80

times that of the poorest

Inflation in Zimbabwe
Rocketing inflation reached 100,000% by early 2008, with almost daily price rises, and shoppers exchanging piles of bank notes for a few groceries, if they could find any food at all.

AUSTRALIA

NEW ZEALAND

20%	19%	18%	17%	15%	15%	13%	11%
Haiti	Honduras	Armenia	Bosnia-Herz.	Nepal	Albania	Philippines	Gambia

There is inequality everywhere. The income of the richest 1 percent of the world's population is equal to the income of the poorest 57 percent. Many people in rich countries live in great poverty, while some people in poor countries live in great wealth. Other kinds of inequality – in power, access to education, recognition of the rights of different groups – are often built on top of the basic income inequity. Measuring the latter thus offers an indication of some of the other potential divisions in a society.

In the hands of the few
Percentage of billionaires
by country of citizenship
2008

There were 1,125 dollar billionaires in 2008.

USA 41%
Russia 8%
China and Hong Kong 6%
Germany 5%
India 5%
Turkey 3%
UK 3%
Canada 2%
Japan 2%
others 25%

USA
In 2008, there were 469 billionaires, and over 51 million people living in poverty.

The richest 100 people own the equivalent of

3%

of the world annual GDP

CANADA

USA

MEXICO
BAHAMAS
HAITI
BELIZE
JAMAICA
DOMINICAN REP.
GUATEMALA
HONDURAS
DOMINICA
EL SALVADOR
NICARAGUA
ST LUCIA
COSTA RICA
VENEZUELA
PANAMA
GUYANA
COLOMBIA
SURINAME
ECUADOR
PERU
BRAZIL
BOLIVIA
PARAGUAY
CHILE
ARGENTINA
URUGUAY

Poor people in rich countries
People whose income is less than half the median income as percentage of population
2000–04
selected countries

19% Russia
17% USA
16% Ireland, Israel
14% Greece, Spain
13% Italy, UK
12% Australia, Estonia, Japan
11% Canada
9% Poland
8% Austria, Germany, Romania, Switzerland
7% France, Hungary, Netherlands Sweden

Inequality

Russia
In 2008, Russia had 87 dollar billionaires, and over 100,000 millionaires, while around 16% of the population lived below subsistence level.

South Africa
There were 49,000 dollar millionaires in South Africa in 2007, a third of them women. The number of super-rich is increasing faster there than almost anywhere else in the world.

Distribution of wealth
latest available 1998–2004
Gini index

The Gini index measures the degree to which the distribution of wealth within a country is different from a perfectly equal distribution. The higher the index, the greater the inequality.

- 50 – 60   *most unequal*
- 40 – 49
- 30 – 39
- 20 – 29   *most equal*
- no data

● unemployment 10% or more
latest available data 1996–2005

6%
Demark, Norway

5%
Czech Republic, Finland

A good guide to the quality of life available in a country is to measure not just wealth but also health and education. The UN's Human Development Index (HDI) does this each year. It reveals the unsurprising insight that, to the extent that quality of life can be measured, richer countries offer more than poor ones. But among both rich and poor countries there are surprises. Some countries seem to be particularly effective at transforming their economic wealth into real benefit for their citizens. Many others are, however, much less effective – either because the political leadership lacks the will to do better, or because the country's history has not included proper investment in the foundations of education and good health care, so it lacks the capacity. Like all national-level statistics, a country's ranking on the HDI may obscure important internal differences. But when a country is ranked much lower on the HDI than its Gross National Income suggests it should be, this is a sign that there are severe social inequalities.

CANADA

USA

BERMUDA

MEXICO

BAHAMAS

CUBA

DOMINICAN REP.

JAMAICA   HAITI

BELIZE

GUATEMALA   HONDURAS

EL SALVADOR   NICARAGUA

ST KITTS & NEVIS

ANTIGUA & BARBUDA

DOMINICA

GRENADA   ST LUCIA

BARBADOS

ST VINCENT & GRENADINES

COSTA RICA

PANAMA

VENEZUELA   TRINIDAD & TOBAGO

GUYANA

SURINAME

COLOMBIA

ECUADOR

PERU

BRAZIL

BOLIVIA

CHILE   PARAGUAY

ARGENTINA

URUGUAY

Healthy water

Percentage of population with access to improved water source
2004 or latest available data

- fewer than 50%
- 50% – 69%
- 70% – 89%
- 90% or more
- no data

The proportion of people with access to a good source of water has increased in about half of all countries since 1990, but has declined in a few.

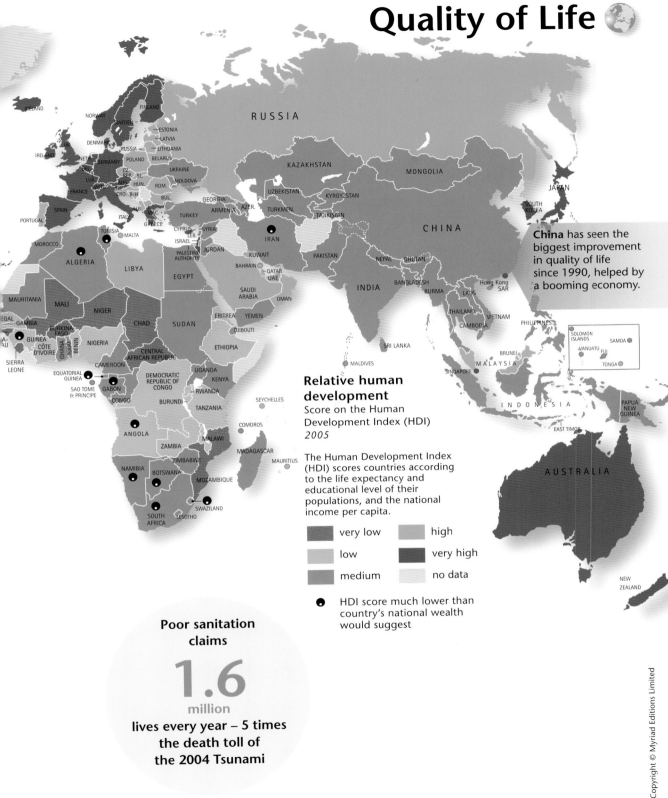

Quality of Life

China has seen the biggest improvement in quality of life since 1990, helped by a booming economy.

Relative human development

Score on the Human Development Index (HDI)
2005

The Human Development Index (HDI) scores countries according to the life expectancy and educational level of their populations, and the national income per capita.

- very low
- low
- medium
- high
- very high
- no data

● HDI score much lower than country's national wealth would suggest

Poor sanitation claims

1.6
million

lives every year – 5 times the death toll of the 2004 Tsunami

CANADA

USA

Venezuela
GNI nearly
equalled in 2006
by sales revenue
of Toyota Motors.

MEXICO

ICELAND

NORWAY   FINLAND
          SWEDEN
                    ESTONIA
IRELAND DENMARK   LATVIA
    UK   RUSSIA   LITHUANIA
         NETH. GERMANY POLAND BELARUS
         BEL.   CZ   UKRAINE
         LUX.   REP. SL.
    FRANCE SWITZ. AUS. HUN.   MOLDOVA
              SL. CRO. R-H SERB. ROM.
            MONT. BUL.
PORTUGAL ITALY ALB. MAC.   GEORGIA
   SPAIN   GREECE TURKEY ARMENIA AZERBAIJAN
                                           TURKMENISTAN

RUSSIA

KAZAKHSTAN

UZBEKISTAN

AFGH.

IRAN

MOROCCO   TUNISIA
                      LEB. SYRIA
              PALESTINE JORDAN
              AUTHORITY
ALGERIA   LIBYA   EGYPT

CAPE
VERDE   MAURITANIA   MALI   NIGER   CHAD   SUDAN   ERITREA YEMEN
SENEGAL   DJIBOUTI
GAMBIA   BURKINA
GUINEA- GUINEA FASO   CENTRAL   ETHIOPIA
BISSAU   CÔTE NIGERIA   AFRICAN REPUBLIC
SIERRA LEONE   D'IVOIRE   UGANDA
   LIBERIA   GHANA BENIN CAMEROON   KENYA
          EQUATORIAL   DEMOCRATIC RWANDA
          GUINEA   REPUBLIC OF BURUNDI
          SAO TOME   CONGO   TANZANIA
          & PRINCIPE GABON

SEYCHELLES

COMOROS

Angola
GNI exceeded in
2006 by the
profits of
ExxonMobil.

ANGOLA   ZAMBIA   MALAWI
                          MADAGASCAR   MAURITIUS
NAMIBIA BOTSWANA   MOZAMBIQUE
                    SWAZILAND
              SOUTH   LESOTHO
              AFRICA

ECUADOR

PERU

BRAZIL

BOLIVIA

PARAGUAY

CHILE   ARGENTINA

URUGUAY

BELIZE
JAMAICA   HAITI DOMINICAN
                  REP.
GUATEMALA HONDURAS   ANTIGUA & BARBUDA
EL SALVADOR   ST KITTS & NEVIS
        NICARAGUA   GRENADA DOMINICA
COSTA RICA   ST LUCIA
   PANAMA VENEZUELA ST VINCENT & GRENADINES
                    TRINIDAD & TOBAGO
   COLOMBIA   GUYANA
              SURINAME

The global mix
Number and status
of corporations located
in country or region
2006 or latest available data

parent corporations

foreign affiliates

9%

USA
27,025

17%

EU
255,630

1%

Southeast Europe & CIS
100,493

5%

Latin America & Caribbean
39,765

10%

Africa
7,142

4%

Asia & Oceania
378,581

Transnationals

Corporate wealth

Gross national income compared with sales revenue of selected transnationals
2006

GNI smaller than sales revenue of:

- Tata Motors ($5.2 billion)
- British Airways ($14.25 billion)
- Hewlett Packard ($94.08 billion)
- Wal-Mart ($348.6 billion)

GNI larger than sales revenue of any transnational

Globalization of the world economy is not new, but it is continually advancing. Transnational corporations have bases in many countries. Their interests reach beyond national loyalties and their wealth far outreaches that of many countries. The sales revenue of Wal-Mart stores in 2006 was close to the GNI of Indonesia – the world's third most populous country – and exceeded the combined GNI of the poorest 49 states.

Thailand
GNI exceeded in 2006 by sales revenue of General Motors.

1.8 million people are employed by Wal-Mart. If each has two dependants, the company is responsible for the well-being of the equivalent of the population of Denmark.

Global players

Corporations with presence in highest number of host countries and location of parent corporation
2007

Value	Company	Location
103	Deutsche Post	Germany
96	Royal Dutch/Shell Group	UK, Netherlands
94	Nestlé	Switzerland
85	Siemens	Germany
84	BASF	Germany
76	Bayer	Germany
74	Citigroup	USA
72	Procter & Gamble	USA
66	IBM	USA
62	Philips Electronics	Netherlands
62	Total	France
62	BP	UK

Foreign Investment

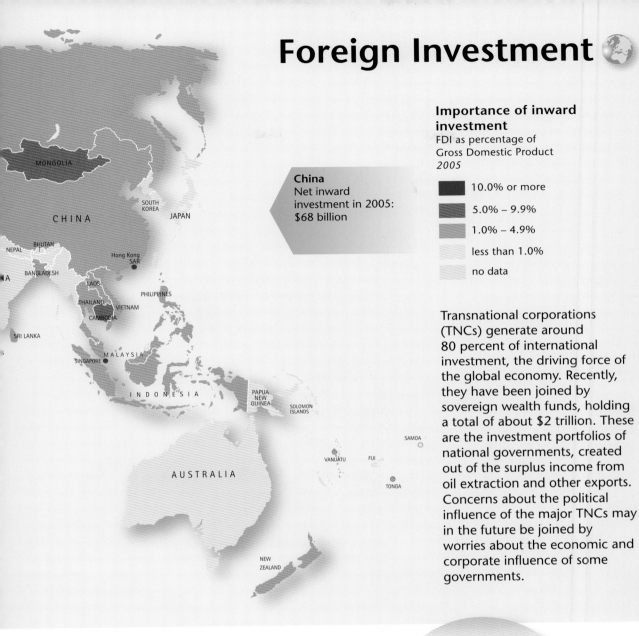

China
Net inward investment in 2005: $68 billion

Importance of inward investment
FDI as percentage of Gross Domestic Product
2005

- 10.0% or more
- 5.0% – 9.9%
- 1.0% – 4.9%
- less than 1.0%
- no data

Transnational corporations (TNCs) generate around 80 percent of international investment, the driving force of the global economy. Recently, they have been joined by sovereign wealth funds, holding a total of about $2 trillion. These are the investment portfolios of national governments, created out of the surplus income from oil extraction and other exports. Concerns about the political influence of the major TNCs may in the future be joined by worries about the economic and corporate influence of some governments.

Attractiveness to investors
UNCTAD assessment of performance and potential
2005–07

- **front-runners:** countries with high FDI potential and performance
- **above potential:** countries with low FDI potential but strong FDI performance
- **below potential:** countries with high FDI potential but low FDI performance
- **under-performers:** countries with both low FDI potential and performance
- no data

Multi-national companies from the larger developing nations are increasingly investing overseas. In 2008, the Indian company Tata bought Jaguar and Land Rover from Ford.

International trade continues to increase, and while comparisons over time are distorted by price inflation, the growth is nonetheless impressive. In recent years, services – actions carried out for money, rather than goods exchanged for money – have become an increasingly important part both of advanced national economies and of world trade. But for almost all countries, traded goods – merchandise – continues to be far more important. Some countries are so dependent on international trade that the combined value of imports and exports exceeds their national income. Yet the USA, which remains a key engine of the world economy, has a relatively low dependence on international trade. This gives it the capacity to recover quickly when the economic cycle turns down.

World trade in merchandise grew from $59 billion in 1948 to $11,783 billion in 2006

Importance of trade

Value of trade as percentage of GDP
2006 or latest data available

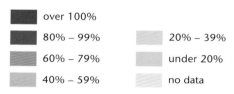

- over 100%
- 80% – 99%
- 60% – 79%
- 40% – 59%
- 20% – 39%
- under 20%
- no data

Merchandise

Trade in services includes the sale of intangible products such as architectural expertise, the provision of a call-centre, or the tourism sector.

Services

Trade

Changing places
Share of total merchandise exported
1948–2006

North America 28% → 28%
Asia 14% → 14% (2006)
14% (1948)

Merchandise exports
by region
2006
US$ billions and percentages

Africa
$352
69% 20%
3%
9%

CIS
$411
65% 25%
4%
7%

South & Central America
$420
42% 31%
24%
2%

Middle East
$633
75% 21%
2%
2%

North America
$1,606
74%
13% 9% 4%

Asia
$3,197
82%
10% 6% 2%

Europe
$4,860
78%
11% 9% 2%

- agricultural products
- fuels and mining products
- manufactured goods
- other

47

Communications technology is essential for business, enabling those with access to tap into the global market. The communications sector itself represents a massive market, with cell-phone revenues in the USA and Japan each worth more than the GDP of around half the countries in the world. Internet-enabled cell phones are contributing substantially to this revenue.

Although internet access is still patchy in low-income countries, where there are few telephone landlines the cell phone is beginning to bridge the communications divide. In 2004, for the first time the number of cell-phone users in non-OECD countries equalled those in OECD countries.

Telephones

Number of fixed lines and cell phone subscribers per 1,000 people
2005

- fewer than 100
- 100 – 499
- 500 – 999
- 1,000 or more
- no data

cell phone subscribers are 90% of total

Where the money is made
Average annual spending by each cell-phone subscriber
2005
selected OECD countries

$232 — Mexico
$293 — Spain
$374 — UK
$506 — USA
$634 — Australia
$860 — Japan

Internet access
Number per 1,000 people
2005

- internet users
- broadband subscribers

523 / 162 — high-income countries
114 / 22 — middle-income countries
44 / 1 — low-income countries

48

Communications

RUSSIA

In Africa, since 2000, the cell-phone network has expanded enormously, covering over a tenth of the population of many countries.

Most popular internet search engines
Total number of searches made
August 2007

Total searches in August 2007:
61 billion

- Google — 37 billion
- Yahoo — 8.5 billion
- Baidu (China) — 3.2 billion
- Microsoft — 2.1 billion
- NHN (South Korea) — 2.0 billion
- eBay — 1.3 billion
- Time Warner — 1.2 billion

Searchers
Number of internet search engine users in each region
August 2007

- Asia-Pacific — 258 million
- Europe — 210 million
- North America — 206 million
- MiddleEast & Africa — 30 million

49

The **USA** is attempting to reduce its heavy reliance on imported fuels by investing in technology to convert plant and waste matter into biofuels.

Germany
Nearly a third of its gas comes from Russia, across Ukraine.

The International Energy Agency predicts an increase in global demand for energy of 50 percent by 2030, much of it from the booming economies of China and India.

The 1959 **Antarctic** Treaty has protected the continent from exploitation, but in the face of faltering oil supplies elsewhere, it may not survive untouched for ever.

ICELAND

NORWAY

SWEDE

UK

DENMARK

RUSS

IRELAND

NETH.

BEL

GERMANY

PO

CANADA

LUX

CZ.
REP.

FRANCE

SWITZ.

AUS.

SL

CRO

B-

USA

PORTUGAL

SPAIN

ITALY

TUNISIA

MAL

MOROCCO

MEXICO

ALGERIA

LIB

CUBA

DOMINICAN
REP.

JAMAICA

HAITI

GUATEMALA

HONDURAS

SENEGAL

EL SALVADOR

NICARAGUA

COSTA RICA

PANAMA

TRINIDAD & TOBAGO

CÔTE
D'IVOIRE

GHANA

TOGO

BENIN

NIGERIA

VENEZUELA

COLOMBIA

CAMEROON

ECUADOR

GABON

CONGO

PERU

BRAZIL

ANGO

BOLIVIA

NAMIBI

PARAGUAY

BOTSWANA

CHILE

ARGENTINA

URUGUAY

Energy Trade

Ukraine relies on Russian-owned Gazprom for half its gas. A price dispute led to Gazprom cutting the supply in 2006.

Russia is claiming an area of the Arctic seabed, possibly rich in oil, gas and minerals. During 2007, it planted a Russian flag on the seabed at the North Pole.

Japan imports more than 80% of its energy.

China is increasing its dependence on imported fuel, with crude oil imports up by 12% in 2007.

RUSSIA

KAZAKHSTAN

UZBEKISTAN

KYRGYZSTAN

GEORGIA

ARMENIA AZERBAIJAN

TURKMENISTAN

TAJIKISTAN

TURKEY

SYRIA

IRAQ

IRAN

PAKISTAN

JORDAN

KUWAIT

BAHRAIN

QATAR

UAE

SAUDI ARABIA

OMAN

YEMEN

JORDAN

ETHIOPIA

KENYA

TANZANIA

MOZAMBIQUE

NEPAL

INDIA

BANGLADESH

BURMA

CHINA

NORTH KOREA

SOUTH KOREA

JAPAN

Hong Kong SAR

THAILAND

VIETNAM

PHILIPPINES

SRI LANKA

BRUNEI

MALAYSIA

INDONESIA

AUSTRALIA

NEW ZEALAND

Who holds the power?
Energy use minus energy production
2004
1,000 tonnes of oil equivalent

Net exporters

 100,000 or more

10,000 – 99,000

fewer than 10,000

Net importers of energy

fewer than 10,000

10,000 – 99,999

100,000 or more

Importance of tourism
Receipts from overseas tourists as percentage of export earnings
2005

- 40% or more
- 20% – 39%
- 10% – 19%
- less than 10%
- no data

Increasing popularity
More than 5 million additional overseas tourists a year
2005, compared with 1995

- 10 million or more *number given*
- 5 million – 9 million

The new-found wealth of many of China's citizens is enabling them to travel overseas. There were 31 million Chinese tourists abroad in 2005, seven times the number in 1995.

KAZAKHSTAN

KYRGYZSTAN

TAJIKISTAN

PAKISTAN

NEPAL

27m
C H I N A

SOUTH KOREA   JAPAN

BANGLADESH

13m

Macao   Hong Kong
SAR   SAR

THAILAND

SRI LANKA   CAMBODIA   VIETNAM   PHILIPPINES

9m   M A L A Y S I A

I N D O N E S I A

The growing recognition of the damage tourism can do to the culture and environment of the places visited, has led to efforts at "responsible tourism."

VANUATU

SAMOA

A U S T R A L I A

Country of origin
Countries generating highest number of overseas tourists
2005

France
22m

FRENCH POLYNESIA

Russian Federation
28m

Malaysia
31m

China
31m

Czech Republic
37m

Poland
41m

USA
64m

UK
66m

Germany
77m

Tourism is fundamental to the economy of many countries but is often a burden on local societies. The most beautiful location cannot sustain tourism without a well-developed transport, energy, water and sanitation infrastructure. As a result, most of the biggest tourist destinations are rich countries.

Tourism

There were
40%
more international tourists in 2005, than in 1995

ICELAND

NORWAY
SWEDEN
FINLAND
ESTONIA
LATVIA
LITHUANIA
BELARUS

6m
UK

7m
RUSSIA
POLAND
GERMANY

12m
RUSSIA

12m
UKRAINE

IRELAND
BEL.
CZ. REP.
AUS.
HUN.
MOLDOVA
ROM.

CANADA

16m
FRANCE
SWITZ.
SL.
B-H
BUL.

13m
GEORGIA
AZERBAIJAN
ARMENIA

21m
PORTUGAL
SPAIN

7m
CROATIA

5m
ITALY
ALB.
MAC.
GREECE
TURKEY
SYRIA

USA

6m

MALTA
CYPRUS
LEB.

MOROCCO
TUNISIA
ISRAEL
JORDAN

5m
EGYPT

6m
SAUDI ARABIA

BAHRAIN

OMAN

MEXICO

Middle East & North Africa
Over 20% of export earnings in the region arise from the tourist industry.

BAHAMAS

JAMAICA
HONDURAS
NICARAGUA

CAPE VERDE

GUATEMALA
EL SALVADOR
COSTA RICA
PANAMA

GAMBIA

BARBADOS

VENEZUELA
GUYANA
SURINAME
COLOMBIA
ECUADOR

GHANA

ETHIOPIA

UGANDA
KENYA

Germany
22m

PERU

BRAZIL

BURUNDI
TANZANIA

SEYCHELLES

Mexico
22m

BOLIVIA

CHILE
PARAGUAY

Country of destination
Countries attracting highest number of overseas tourists
2005

MOZAMBIQUE

MAURITIUS

Russian Federation
22m

ARGENTINA
URUGUAY

SOUTH AFRICA

Hong Kong, China
23m

UK
30m

Italy
37m

China
47m

USA
49m

Spain
56m

France
76m

Tourism often threatens the natural and architectural beauty that attracts the visitors. It is a potent form of cultural invasion, and in extreme circumstances armed groups have declared tourists to be legitimate targets for attack.

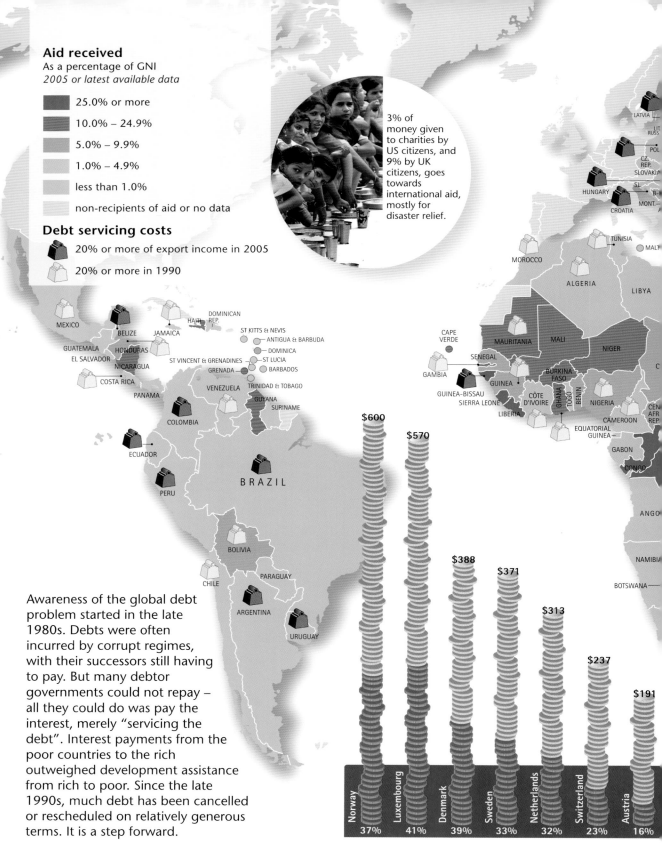

Aid received

As a percentage of GNI
2005 or latest available data

- 25.0% or more
- 10.0% – 24.9%
- 5.0% – 9.9%
- 1.0% – 4.9%
- less than 1.0%
- non-recipients of aid or no data

3% of money given to charities by US citizens, and 9% by UK citizens, goes towards international aid, mostly for disaster relief.

Debt servicing costs

- 20% or more of export income in 2005
- 20% or more in 1990

Awareness of the global debt problem started in the late 1980s. Debts were often incurred by corrupt regimes, with their successors still having to pay. But many debtor governments could not repay – all they could do was pay the interest, merely "servicing the debt". Interest payments from the poor countries to the rich outweighed development assistance from rich to poor. Since the late 1990s, much debt has been cancelled or rescheduled on relatively generous terms. It is a step forward.

Norway	Luxembourg	Denmark	Sweden	Netherlands	Switzerland	Austria
$600	$570	$388	$371	$313	$237	$191
37%	41%	39%	33%	32%	23%	16%

54

Debt and Aid

Official development assistance

Amount donated per capita and percentage going to least developed countries
2005
US$

- total government ODA per capita
- percentage of total going to least developed countries

In 2000, the world's richest countries pledged to be spending 0.7% of their national income on aid by 2015. Only five countries – Denmark, Luxembourg, Netherlands, Norway and Sweden – were at that level by 2005.

Country	ODA per capita	% to least developed
Belgium	$188	31%
Ireland	$180	51%
UK	$179	25%
Finland	$171	27%
France	$165	24%
Germany	$122	19%
Canada	$116	28%
Japan	$103	18%
USA	$93	21%
Italy	$87	28%
Australia	$83	25%
Spain	$70	27%
New Zealand	$67	25%
Portugal	$36	56%
Greece	$35	21%

55

Graffiti on the wall of the Dheisheh Camp, Bethlehem, in the Occupied West Bank. Established by the UN in 1948, it is home to 11,000 Palestinians.

Part Three: War and Peace

This is an era of growing peace, despite the war horrors that persist in Afghanistan, Darfur in Sudan, Iraq, and other regions. The frequency and lethality of wars has been declining since the end of the Cold War in 1989. Most wars since the end of World War II have been within states, or between states and their colonies, rather than between recognized states. That the world in general is getting safer is, however, no comfort to those who daily face extreme insecurity and living conditions in which brutality is part of the reality.

USA

UK

RUS*

MACEDO*

ALGERIA

NIGER

SENEGAL

GUINEA

CÔTE
D'IVOIRE

SIERRA
LEONE

GHANA

NIGERIA

LIBERIA

C*
AF
RE

HAITI

COLOMBIA

ANGO

NAM*

Progress towards peace
Number of wars
1990, 2000, 2007

	1990
	2000
	2007

**Central &
South America**

6

1

1

Europe

4

2

2

Sub-Saharan Africa

18

20

12

**Middle East &
North Africa**

7

4

3

Asia & the Pacific

21

20

16

War in the 21st century

RUSSIA

GEORGIA

TURKEY

LEBANON

IRAQ

AFGHANISTAN

PALESTINE
AUTHORITY

PAKISTAN

NEPAL

INDIA

Wars in 1990:

56

Wars in 2007:

34

BURMA

THAILAND

PHILIPPINES

SRI LANKA

SUDAN

ERITREA

ETHIOPIA

UGANDA

SOMALIA

RWANDA

BURUNDI

INDONESIA

SOLOMON
ISLANDS

ZIMBABWE

Experience of war
Open armed conflict
with continuity
between clashes
2000–07

experienced armed conflict

 armed conflict(s) ongoing in 2007

 also fought in war(s)
outside national border

 only fought in war(s)
outside national border

AUSTRALIA

Child soldiers
2001–05

used in active combat by militias

RUSSIA

ISRAEL
PALESTINE AUTHORITY
IRAQ
AFGHANISTAN
BURMA
PHILIPPINES

COLOMBIA
LIBERIA
CÔTE D'IVOIRE
CHAD
SUDAN
CENTRAL AFRICAN REP.
UGANDA
SOMALIA
SRI LANKA
DEM. REP. OF CONGO
BURUNDI
ANGOLA
INDONESIA

Non-state wars occur where the state has a limited capacity to impose order – or has simply collapsed. This may happen alongside one or more internal wars. In some cases, the guerrillas and paramilitaries are supported by the government and used as deniable instruments of policy. In other cases, factions within the government support one side as part of their internal power struggle.

In all cases, the civilian population suffers. Although governments are capable of great brutality, most campaigns of violence against civilians are carried out by non-state forces. One form of abuse, in which militias lead the way though governments are also culpable, is forcing children to fight, often brutalizing them to reduce their resistance to committing violence. When peace returns, helping former child soldiers find a normal life is a delicate and challenging task.

Non-state wars
2002–07

at least one armed conflict in which no state is involved

MEXICO
GUATEMALA
COLOMBIA
ECUADOR
BRAZIL
SENE

Colombia United Self-Defence Forces – broadly, pro-government, often organized by major landowners – against various leftwing groups, the largest being the Revolutionary Armed Forces of Colombia (FARC).

Campaigns of violence against civilian populations
Number of campaigns by perpetrator
1989–2005

— non-state armed groups
— governments

Warlords and Militias 🌐

There are some wars – fought, as others are, for control of territory, resources or power – in which neither party is a state. Most of the fighting in Somalia since 1991 is a case in point. The parties to these wars are armed guerrilla groups and militias. These conflicts have only recently been recognized as a serious international problem, so information on them is patchy and does not go back very far.

AFGHANISTAN

IRAQ

PALESTINE AUTHORITY

PAKISTAN

NEPAL

INDIA

BANGLADESH

BURMA

CHAD

SUDAN

NIGERIA

ETHIOPIA

SOMALIA

PHILIPPINES

SRI LANKA

DEMOCRATIC REPUBLIC OF CONGO

UGANDA

KENYA

BURUNDI

INDONESIA

Somalia
Multiple groups, some in loose affiliations with others. Union of Islamic Courts started to form a government, but was blocked by US-backed Ethiopian intervention.

Sri Lanka
Liberation Tigers of Tamil Eelam against the breakaway, pro-government Karuna faction.

Dem. Rep. of Congo
Multiple small and large armed groups – most made up of Congolese of different tribes, and some of Rwandan groups implicated in the 1994 genocide.

Around 50% of all armed conflicts are between warlords and armed militias and do not involve government forces.

Number of non-state wars
by region
2002–05

2002	2003
2004	2005

Americas
2 2 4 3

Sub-Saharan Africa
24 23 17 14

Middle East & North Africa
3 3 3 3

Central and South Asia
3 5 3 4

East & South-East Asia & Oceania
2 1 1

61

From 2002 to 2007, there was an increase in recorded terrorist incidents of

750%

New York and Washington DC, USA, September 2001

Al Qaida terrorists crash three airliners into the World Trade Centre and the Pentagon, killing 2,973 people of more than 50 nationalities.

London, UK, July 2005

Four suicide bombers on public transport kill 52 people.

USA

Madrid, Spain, March 2004

Bombs on four trains kill 191 people.

UK

SPAIN

Israel/Palestine

Since 2000, Palestinian groups have used suicide bombings and rocket attacks against occupation by Israel, which responds with targeted killings, rocket strikes and army offensives. By 2007, 1,031 Israelis had been killed, 70% of them civilians. Of the 5,102 Palestinians killed, around half were not involved in the campaign.

ALGERIA

Algeria, 2007

At least 150 people killed in campaign by al Qaida group.

Terrorism is a form of warfare – not an ideology but an instrument by which some groups try to advance their cause. The kind of attack usually described as terrorist is used predominantly by the weaker party, which may not have access to missiles, gunships and tanks. Governments, however, have also made covert use of terror tactics. Contemporary suicide bombing was pioneered by Tamil secessionists in Sri Lanka, but its most widespread use has been in the Middle East.

Terrorism

Moscow, Russia, October 2002

50 Chechen fighters hold 700 theatre-goers hostage. Rescue raid by Russian forces kills Chechens and over 100 hostages.

Beslan, Russia, September 2004

Chechen fighters hold children and parents hostage in school. 336 hostages and 30 Chechens killed when Russian security forces storm school.

Baghdad, Iraq, August 2005

1,000 people die in human stampede when a rumoured sighting of a suicide bomber causes panic among Shi'a pilgrims.

Ramadi & Fallujah, Iraq, March 2007

Insurgents detonate trucks filled with chlorine gas.

Gujarat, India, 2002

29 Hindu worshippers shot dead by unknown gunmen.

RUSSIA

LEBANON
ISRAEL
IRAQ
PAKISTAN
EGYPT
SAUDI ARABIA
INDIA

Pakistan, 2007

Karachi, October
Bomb kills 140 supporters of ex-Prime Minister Benazir Bhutto on her return from exile.
Rawalpindi, December
Bhutto and 28 supporters killed in further attack.

Beirut, Lebanon, February 2005

Bomb kills former Prime Minister Rafiq Hariri and 20 others.

KENYA

SRI LANKA

Riyadh, Saudi Arabia, May 2003

Suicide bomber kills 26 in attack on western housing complex.

INDONESIA

Bali, Indonesia, October 2002

200 holidaymakers killed in al Qaida bomb attack.

50%
of 14,500 recorded terrorist incidents in 2007 were in Iraq

Mombasa, Kenya, 2002

Al Qaida suicide bomb attack on hotel kills 3 Israelis and 10 Kenyans.

Sri Lanka, 1980s–2008

The Liberation Tigers of Tamil Eelam have killed, among others: a president of Sri Lanka; a former Prime Minister of India; 40 Sri Lankan politicians.

Red Sea coast, Egypt

Sharm el-Sheikh, 2005: 88 dead
Dahab, 2006: 23 dead.

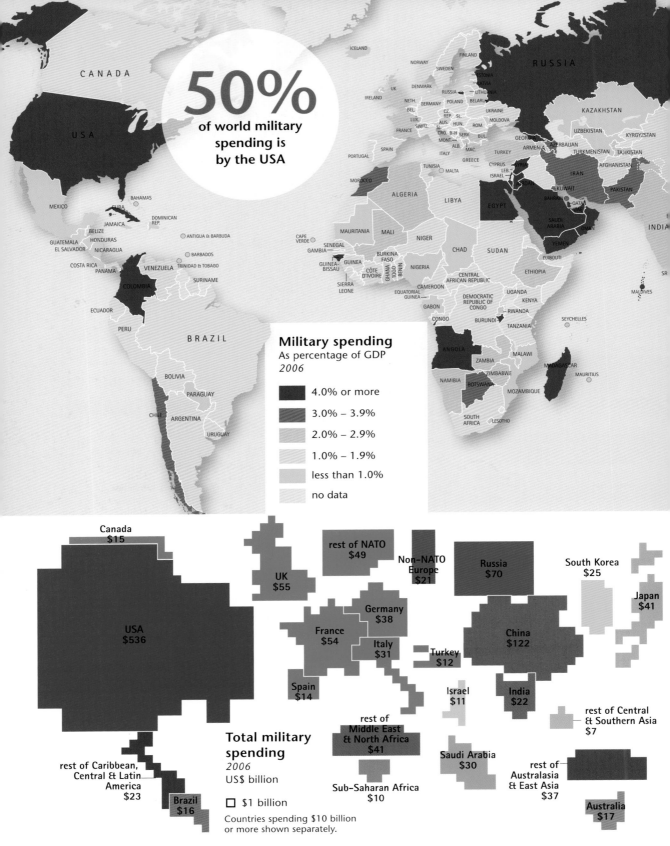

50%
of world military spending is by the USA

Military spending
As percentage of GDP
2006

- 4.0% or more
- 3.0% – 3.9%
- 2.0% – 2.9%
- 1.0% – 1.9%
- less than 1.0%
- no data

Total military spending
2006
US$ billion

☐ $1 billion

Countries spending $10 billion or more shown separately.

Canada $15

rest of NATO $49

Non-NATO Europe $21

Russia $70

South Korea $25

UK $55

Japan $41

USA $536

Germany $38

France $54

China $122

Italy $31

Turkey $12

Israel $11

India $22

Spain $14

rest of Central & Southern Asia $7

rest of Caribbean, Central & Latin America $23

rest of Middle East & North Africa $41

Saudi Arabia $30

rest of Australasia & East Asia $37

Brazil $16

Sub-Saharan Africa $10

Australia $17

Military Spending

Global military spending rose by 35 percent from 1997 to 2007 and at over $1.1 trillion a year is now close to the level at the height of the Cold War in the 1980s. At the start of the 1990s, with the Cold War over, many countries achieved a major redirection of resources into the civilian economy. Following small increases at the end of the 1990s, US military spending accelerated dramatically after the terrorist attacks of September 11, 2001 and with the invasion and occupation of Iraq. The USA now dominates world military spending to an unprecedented degree.

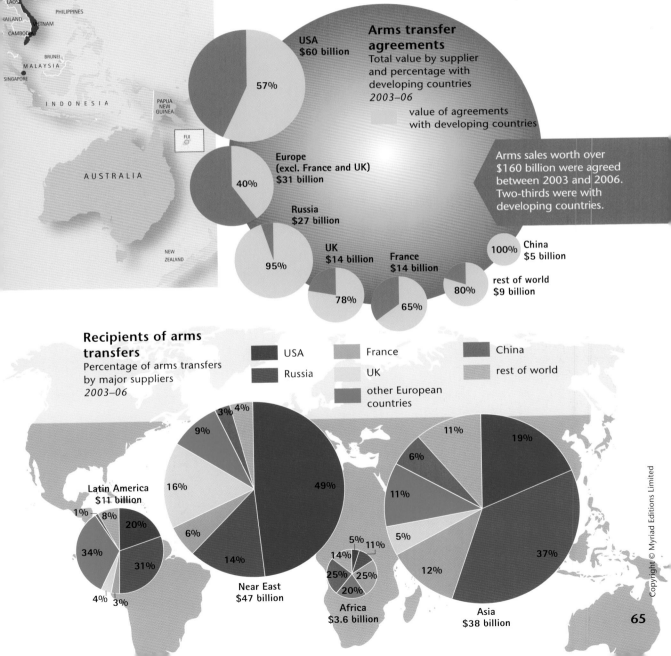

Arms transfer agreements
Total value by supplier and percentage with developing countries
2003–06

value of agreements with developing countries

USA
$60 billion
57%

Europe
(excl. France and UK)
$31 billion
40%

Russia
$27 billion
95%

UK
$14 billion
78%

France
$14 billion
65%

rest of world
$9 billion
80%

China
$5 billion
100%

Arms sales worth over $160 billion were agreed between 2003 and 2006. Two-thirds were with developing countries.

Recipients of arms transfers
Percentage of arms transfers by major suppliers
2003–06

USA
Russia
France
UK
other European countries
China
rest of world

Latin America
$11 billion
8% 20% 31% 3% 4% 34% 1% 16% 9%

Near East
$47 billion
49% 14% 6% 16% 9% 3% 4%

Africa
$3.6 billion
11% 5% 25% 20% 25% 14%

Asia
$38 billion
19% 37% 12% 5% 11% 6% 11%

65

SWEDEN
NORWAY FINLAND
DENMARK
LATVIA
LITHUANIA
IRELAND
UK
NETH.
POLAND
BELARUS
RUSSIA
1,027,000
CANADA
BELGIUM
GERMANY
UKRAINE
CZ. REP.
SLO.
GEORGIA
AZ
SWITZ. AUSTRIA HUN.
A
FRANCE
255,000
SL
ROMANIA
MOLDOVA
CRO.
USA
1,498,000
ITALY
SERB.
B-H
BULGARIA
TURKEY
510,000
MONT.
MAC.
ALB.
SPAIN
GREECE
PORTUGAL
CYPRUS
MEXICO
S
29
LEBANON
CUBA
TUNISIA
DOMINICAN REP.
MOROCCO
LIBYA
GUATEMALA
HONDURAS
ALGERIA
NIGER
EGYPT
469,000
EL SALVADOR
NICARAGUA
ISRAEL
JOR
VENEZUELA
SENEGAL MAURITANIA
MALI
NIGERIA
COLOMBIA
254,000
GUINEA-BISSAU
GUINEA
BURKINA FASO
SIERRA LEONE
CÔTE D'IVOIRE
BENIN
CHAD
SUDAN
ECUADOR
GHANA
TOGO
CAMEROON
ERITREA
DJIB
PERU
BRAZIL
368,000
GABON
ETHIOPIA
UGANDA
CONGO
KENYA
DEM. REP. OF CONGO
RWANDA
TAN
PARAGUAY
BURUNDI MALAWI
BOLIVIA
URUGUAY
ZAMBIA
MOZAMBIQUE
CHILE ARGENTINA
ANGOLA
ZIMBABWE
NAMIBIA
BOTSWANA
SOUTH AFRICA
MADAGASC

Warlords and militias
Estimated number
in non-state groups
where known
2008

🏃 10,000 or more

🏃 fewer than 10,000

RUSSIA
RUSSIA
SERBIA
MOLDOVA
UZBEKISTAN
SPAIN
TURKEY
LEBANON
AFGHANISTAN
ISRAEL
IRAQ
PALESTINE AUTHORITY
JORDAN
IRAN
PAKISTAN
WESTERN SAHARA
ALGERIA
LIBYA
EGYPT
INDIA
BANGLADESH
BURMA LAOS
SENEGAL
NIGER
ERITREA
YEMEN
PHILIPPINES
CÔTE D'IVOIRE
NIGERIA
CENTRAL AFRICAN REPUBLIC
SUDAN
ETHIOPIA
THAILAND
COLOMBIA
SOMALIA
SRI LANKA
UGANDA
PERU
DEM. REP. OF CONGO
BURUNDI
I N D O N E S I A

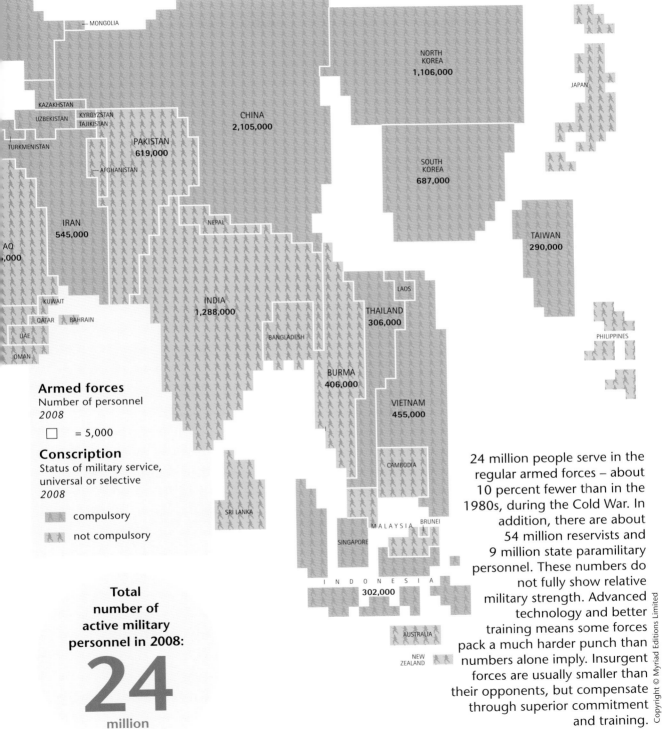

MONGOLIA

KAZAKHSTAN

UZBEKISTAN

KYRGYZSTAN

TAJIKISTAN

TURKMENISTAN

PAKISTAN
619,000

AFGHANISTAN

CHINA
2,105,000

NORTH
KOREA
1,106,000

JAPAN

SOUTH
KOREA
687,000

IRAN
545,000

NEPAL

TAIWAN
290,000

AQ
,000

INDIA
1,288,000

LAOS

KUWAIT

QATAR   BAHRAIN

UAE

OMAN

BANGLADESH

THAILAND
306,000

PHILIPPINES

BURMA
406,000

VIETNAM
455,000

Armed forces
Number of personnel
2008

☐ = 5,000

Conscription
Status of military service,
universal or selective
2008

compulsory

not compulsory

CAMBODIA

SRI LANKA

MALAYSIA   BRUNEI

SINGAPORE

I N D O N E S I A
302,000

AUSTRALIA

NEW
ZEALAND

**Total
number of
active military
personnel in 2008:**

24
million

24 million people serve in the
regular armed forces – about
10 percent fewer than in the
1980s, during the Cold War. In
addition, there are about
54 million reservists and
9 million state paramilitary
personnel. These numbers do
not fully show relative
military strength. Advanced
technology and better
training means some forces
pack a much harder punch than
numbers alone imply. Insurgent
forces are usually smaller than
their opponents, but compensate
through superior commitment
and training.

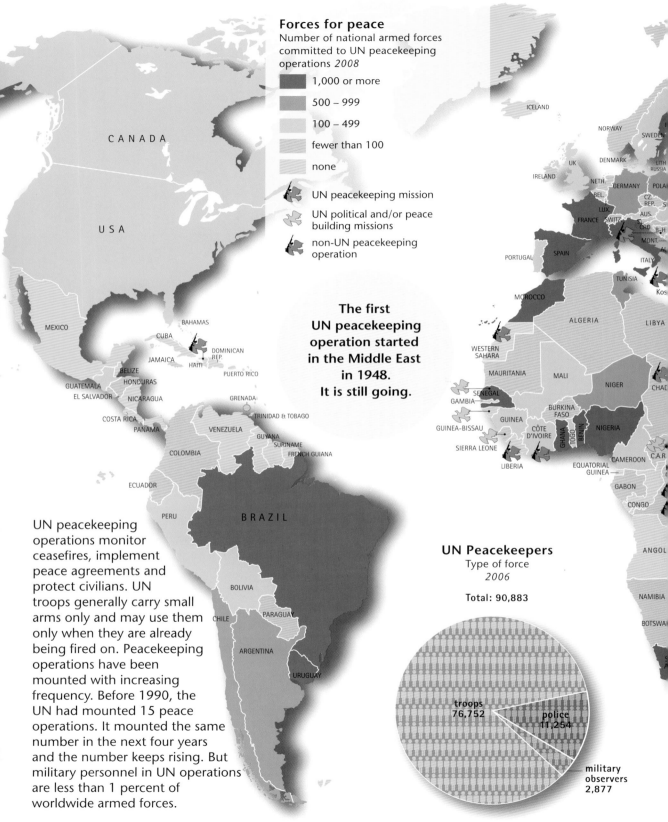

Forces for peace

Number of national armed forces committed to UN peacekeeping operations *2008*

- 1,000 or more
- 500 – 999
- 100 – 499
- fewer than 100
- none

- UN peacekeeping mission
- UN political and/or peace building missions
- non-UN peacekeeping operation

The first
UN peacekeeping
operation started
in the Middle East
in 1948.
It is still going.

CANADA

USA

MEXICO

BAHAMAS

CUBA

JAMAICA   DOMINICAN REP.

HAITI

PUERTO RICO

GUATEMALA   BELIZE
EL SALVADOR   HONDURAS
               NICARAGUA

COSTA RICA

PANAMA

GRENADA

TRINIDAD & TOBAGO

COLOMBIA

VENEZUELA

GUYANA

SURINAME

FRENCH GUIANA

ECUADOR

PERU

BRAZIL

BOLIVIA

CHILE

PARAGUAY

ARGENTINA

URUGUAY

ICELAND

NORWAY   SWEDEN

DENMARK

UK   LITH
        RUSSIA

IRELAND

NETH.

GERMANY   POLA

BEL

CZ. REP.

LUX

AUS.

FRANCE   SWITZ.

CRO
B-H
MONT.
AL

PORTUGAL

SPAIN

ITALY

TUNISIA

Kos

MOROCCO

ALGERIA   LIBYA

WESTERN SAHARA

MAURITANIA   MALI   NIGER   CHAD

SENEGAL

GAMBIA

GUINEA   BURKINA FASO

GUINEA-BISSAU

SIERRA LEONE   CÔTE D'IVOIRE

GHANA   TOGO   BENIN

NIGERIA

LIBERIA   EQUATORIAL GUINEA

CAMEROON   C.A.R

GABON

CONGO

ANGOL

NAMIBIA

BOTSWA

UN peacekeeping operations monitor ceasefires, implement peace agreements and protect civilians. UN troops generally carry small arms only and may use them only when they are already being fired on. Peacekeeping operations have been mounted with increasing frequency. Before 1990, the UN had mounted 15 peace operations. It mounted the same number in the next four years and the number keeps rising. But military personnel in UN operations are less than 1 percent of worldwide armed forces.

UN Peacekeepers

Type of force
2006

Total: 90,883

troops
76,752

police
11,254

military observers
2,877

Peacekeeping

2,425
UN peacekeepers
died between 1948
and the end of 2007.

RUSSIA

KAZAKHSTAN

MONGOLIA

NORTH KOREA

JAPAN

SOUTH KOREA

UZBEKISTAN

KYRGYZSTAN

GEORGIA

AZER.

ARMENIA

TURKEY

TURKMENISTAN

TAJIKISTAN

AFGHANISTAN

CHINA

see inset below

IRAN

KUWAIT

BAHRAIN

QATAR

UAE

PAKISTAN

NEPAL

BHUTAN

BANGLADESH

BURMA

TAIWAN

GYPT

SAUDI ARABIA

OMAN

INDIA

LAOS

SUDAN

ERITREA

YEMEN

THAILAND

PHILIPPINES

VIETNAM

VANUATU

FIJI

SAMOA

DJIBOUTI

fur

ETHIOPIA

CAMBODIA

PALAU

UGANDA

SOMALIA

SRI LANKA

BRUNEI

M A L A Y S I A

RWANDA

KENYA

SINGAPORE

TANZANIA

CYPRUS

LEBANON

SYRIA

DI

ISRAEL

IRAQ

I N D O N E S I A

PAPUA NEW GUINEA

BIA

MALAWI

PALESTINE AUTHORITY

JORDAN

EAST TIMOR

ABWE

MADAGASCAR

West Bank

MOZAMBIQUE

SWAZILAND

AUSTRALIA

SOTHO

UN peacekeeping missions
Number ongoing
1950–2008

2

1950

4

1960

4

1970

6

1980

10

1990

18

2000

20

2008

NEW ZEALAND

Far more information is available about wars today than only a few years ago. But one thing we do not know is how many people are killed. As researchers unearth more information, we discover how little we still know about human suffering in war.

The reasons for this uncertainty include the remote locations of much of the suffering, lack of interest by the international news media, deliberate deception and concealment by the parties to war.

10 million

or more people died in battle 1946–2005

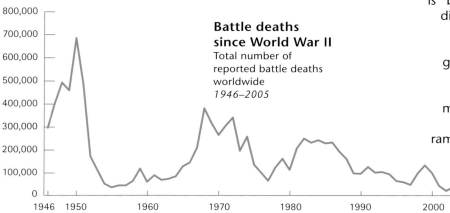

Battle deaths since World War II
Total number of reported battle deaths worldwide
1946–2005

One measure of violence in war is "battle deaths" – people killed directly in combat. It does not include all people who die violently in war – such as in genocide – nor those who die because doctors have been killed, hospitals destroyed, medical supplies seized, crops devastated – all leading to rampant disease and starvation. Though incomplete, battle death numbers do reveal something important: the world has been getting less dangerous. There were 2.3 million battle deaths in the first five years after World War II, but in the five years between 2001 and 2005, battle deaths were 95 percent lower.

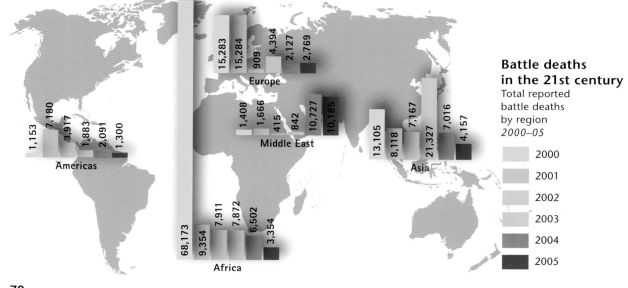

Battle deaths in the 21st century
Total reported battle deaths by region
2000–05

2000
2001
2002
2003
2004
2005

Americas: 1,153 7,180 3,917 1,883 2,091 1,300

Europe: 15,283 15,284 909 4,394 2,127 2,769

Middle East: 1,408 1,666 415 842 10,727 10,185

Asia: 13,105 8,118 7,167 21,327 7,016 4,157

Africa: 68,173 9,354 7,911 7,872 6,502 3,354

The lack of war casualty figures that are both accurate and generally accepted is reflected in the discrepancies of 10:1 in estimates of the death toll in Iraq since March 2003. And views about the rights and wrongs of the US-led occupation of Iraq are inevitably coloured by estimates about the human costs. Such discrepancies in death tolls are not unusual, and are apparent in the range of figures given for many recent conflicts.

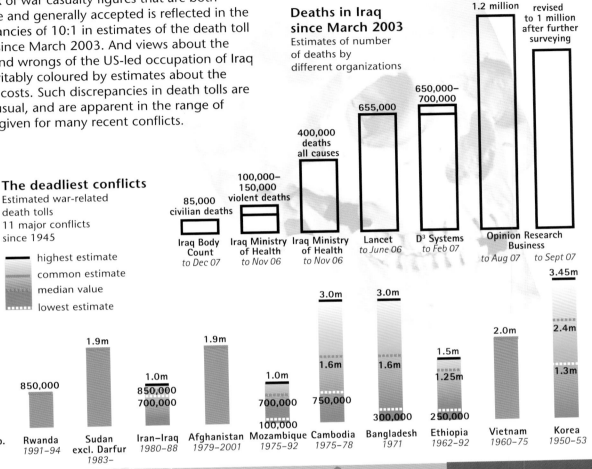

Deaths in Iraq since March 2003
Estimates of number of deaths by different organizations

- 85,000 civilian deaths — **Iraq Body Count** *to Dec 07*
- 100,000–150,000 violent deaths — **Iraq Ministry of Health** *to Nov 06*
- 400,000 deaths all causes — **Iraq Ministry of Health** *to Nov 06*
- 655,000 — **Lancet** *to June 06*
- 650,000–700,000 — **D³ Systems** *to Feb 07*
- 1.2 million — **Opinion Research Business** *to Aug 07*
- revised to 1 million after further surveying — **Research** *to Sept 07*

The deadliest conflicts
Estimated war-related death tolls
11 major conflicts since 1945

- highest estimate
- common estimate
- median value
- lowest estimate

- **5.4m** — Dem. Rep. Congo *1998–*
- **850,000** — Rwanda *1991–94*
- **1.9m** — Sudan excl. Darfur *1983–*
- **1.0m / 850,000 / 700,000** — Iran–Iraq *1980–88*
- **1.9m** — Afghanistan *1979–2001*
- **1.0m / 700,000 / 100,000** — Mozambique *1975–92*
- **3.0m / 1.6m / 750,000** — Cambodia *1975–78*
- **3.0m / 1.6m / 300,000** — Bangladesh *1971*
- **1.5m / 1.25m / 250,000** — Ethiopia *1962–92*
- **2.0m** — Vietnam *1960–75*
- **3.45m / 2.4m / 1.3m** — Korea *1950–53*

1,367 people were reported killed by landmines in 2006

Persistent killers
Countries experiencing casualties from landmines and/or Explosive Remnants of War *2006*

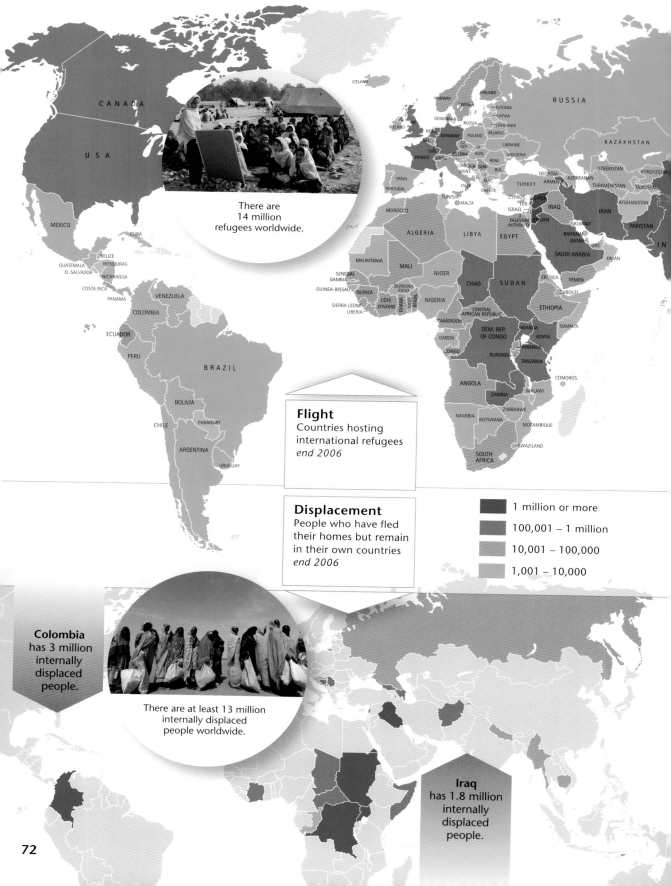

There are
14 million
refugees worldwide.

Flight
Countries hosting
international refugees
end 2006

Displacement
People who have fled
their homes but remain
in their own countries
end 2006

1 million or more

100,001 – 1 million

10,001 – 100,000

1,001 – 10,000

Colombia
has 3 million
internally
displaced
people.

There are at least 13 million
internally displaced
people worldwide.

Iraq
has 1.8 million
internally
displaced
people.

Refugees

27 million people who have fled war or repression are unable to return to their homes; many have been forced to flee more than once. Neglect of these people is reflected in the unsatisfactory and inconsistent statistics about them – very nearly as poor as statistics on the casualties of war. While a well-respected independent US organization counts 99 countries as hosting refugees, the UN identifies 163 host countries. From one source to another the number of refugees hosted by the USA varies by a ratio of 6:1, and for those hosted by the UK the variation is 15:1.

Major refugee populations
Origin and place of refuge
end 2006 or latest available data

**Palestinians
4.3 million**

internal
1.65 million

Jordan
1.8 million

Syria
425,000

Lebanon
400,000

**Iraqis
3.2 million**

other
180,000

Jordan
500,000

Syria
700,000

internal
1.8 million

Iran
54,000

**Afghans
2.2 million**

internal
130,000

other
120,000

Iran
914,000

Pakistan
1 million

**Sudanese
2 million**

other
88,000

Chad
233,000

Uganda
216,000

Kenya
73,000

Ethiopia
67,000

internal
1.3 million

**Congolese (Dem. Rep.)
1.4 million**

other
184,000

Tanzania
128,000

Zambia
61,000

internal
1 million

Statelessness
Countries with populations of stateless persons
end 2006

101 – 1,000

fewer than 100

no data

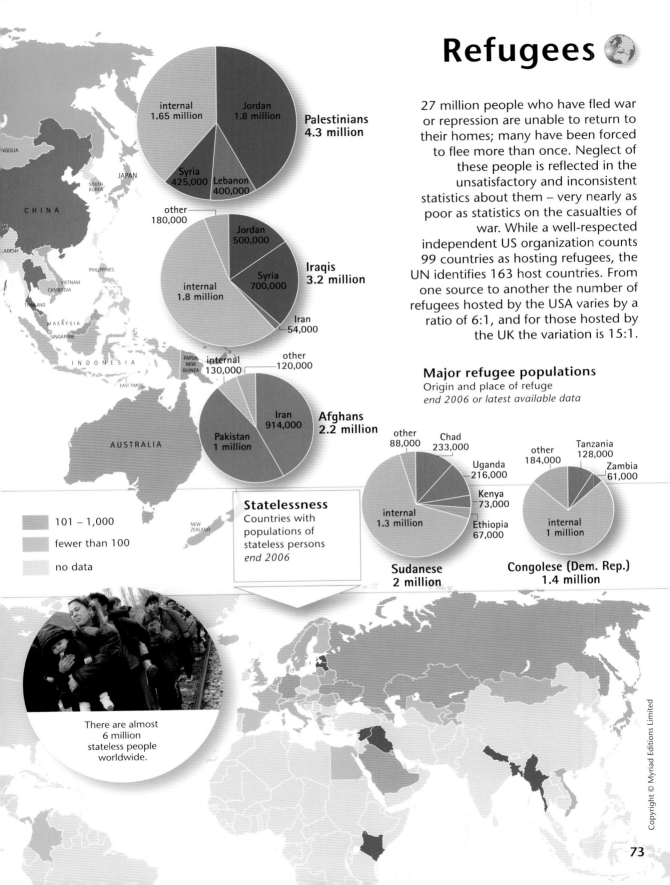

There are almost 6 million stateless people worldwide.

Nordic peace
Denmark, Finland, Iceland, Norway, Sweden have low crime rates, good relations with each other, and small armed forces used abroad only for UN peacekeeping.

North American contrast
The USA scores poorly because of its engagement in wars, its high military spending, social violence and prison population. Canada is more peaceful at home; its forces are used only for UN peacekeeping.

Change in Latin America
Both Chile and Argentina are former dictatorships that went through years of violent political repression. The rise of peace in the past two decades is striking.

Angolan rise
Angola's GPI score improved substantially from 2007 to 2008, reflecting its continuing recovery from its struggle for independence, followed by 27 years of civil war that ended in 2002.

CANADA

USA

MEXICO

CUBA

JAMAICA HAITI DOMINICAN REP.

GUATEMALA
EL SALVADOR HONDURAS
NICARAGUA

COSTA RICA
PANAMA

VENEZUELA

COLOMBIA

ECUADOR

PERU

BRAZIL

BOLIVIA

PARAGUAY

CHILE ARGENTINA

URUGUAY

ICELAND

NORWAY SWEDEN

UK DENMARK LITHUAN
RUSSIA

IRELAND NETH. POLAN
BEL GERMANY
LUX. CZ.
REP.
FRANCE SWITZ. AUS. HU
SI
CRO. B-H
AL

PORTUGAL SPAIN ITALY

TUNISIA

MOROCCO

ALGERIA LIBY

WESTERN
SAHARA

MAURITANIA MALI

SENEGAL

BURKINA
FASO CHA

CÔTE
D'IVOIRE GHANA NIGERIA

CAMEROON CE
AFRIC

EQUATORIAL
GUINEA GABON

CONGO R
C

ANGO

NAMIBIA

BOTSWA

SI
A

Global Peace

Level of peacefulness
According to Global Peace
Index (GPI)
2008

- very high
- high
- medium
- low
- very low
- no data

South Asia
Pakistan's low GPI score reflects high levels of violence internally, tense relations with India despite efforts to ease them, and the overflow of violence from Afghanistan.

Discussion of armed conflict and peace almost always focuses heavily on conflict and violence – what goes wrong and why. The Global Peace Index is an independent attempt to make sense of the other, too often neglected, part of the discussion – what goes right and why. The Index ranks countries according to their peacefulness, looking both at peace at home (government stability, democratic values, community relations and trust between citizens) and peace in foreign relations (military spending, commitment to UN operations and avoidance of war).

The Index is based on the idea that helping people and governments to understand what creates peaceful relations is a significant step towards making it possible for the world to be more peaceful.

75

On a wall in Senegal a message of hope – "Espoirs".

Political systems
2008

- established democracy
- weak, uncertain or transitional democracy
- effective or formal one-party rule
- military dictatorship
- monarchy or theocracy
- state of disorder
- dependent territory

average voter turnout below 50% 1945–2007

Of the 20 states at the top of the UN Human Development Index, all are established democracies.

Until the 1990s, most Central and South American countries experienced extended periods of military rule and civil war.

Of the 20 states at the bottom of the UN Human Development Index, only two are established democracies.

For a state to be counted as a stable democracy, free and fair elections between independent political parties must be the established means of deciding who holds executive power, and the handover of power from one party to another as a result of elections must be peaceful. It often takes several elections and many years before democracy is properly established. Until then it is vulnerable to corruption, incompetence, nepotism and the temptations of authoritarian rule.

43%
of people live
in established
democracies

RUSSIA

KAZAKHSTAN

MONGOLIA

UZBEKISTAN

KYRGYZSTAN

NORTH
KOREA

JAPAN

GEORGIA

ARMENIA   AZER.

TURKMEN.

TAJIKISTAN

SOUTH
KOREA

SYRIA

AFGHANISTAN

CHINA

EB.

IRAQ   IRAN

PAKISTAN

TAIWAN

JORDAN

KUWAIT

NEPAL   BHUTAN

BAHRAIN

QATAR
UAE

SAUDI ARABIA   OMAN

INDIA

BANGLADESH

BURMA

LAOS

PHILIPPINES

VIETNAM

ERITREA
YEMEN

CAMBODIA

ETHIOPIA

DJIBOUTI

SRI LANKA

THAILAND

BRUNEI

MALDIVES

MALAYSIA

UGANDA   SOMALIA

SINGAPORE

RWANDA   KENYA

INDONESIA

PAPUA
NEW
GUINEA

BURUNDI

SEYCHELLES

TANZANIA

SOLOMON
ISLANDS

COMOROS

EAST TIMOR

MALAWI

MADAGASCAR

MAURITIUS

MOZAMBIQUE

AUSTRALIA

SWAZILAND

THO

MICRONESIA,
FED. STATES OF

NAURU   KIRIBATI

TUVALU

VANUATU

FIJI

NEW
CALEDONIA

TONGA

FRENCH
POLYNESIA

NEW
ZEALAND

One person, one vote
is a fundamental principle of
democracy. Thumbprints can be
scanned by computer to
identify voter fraud.

The population of Turkey is more than 97% Muslim, but its legal system draws on Swiss, Italian, French and German civil codes, introduced in 1926.

ICELAND
Lutheranism *Christianity*

Lutheranism *Christianity*

Lutheranism Orthodox Church of Finland *Christianity*

SWEDEN
FINLAND

NORWAY

Church of England Church of Scotland *Christianity*

RUSSIA

ESTONIA
LATVIA
LITHUANIA
RUSSIA

Lutheranism *Christianity*

DENMARK

BELARUS

IRELAND
UK
NETH.
BELGIUM
GERMANY
POLAND
UKRAINE

Roman Catholicism Judaism Islam Protestantism Anglicanism Orthodox Church Secularism

LUX.
LIECHT.
FRANCE
SWITZ.
CZECH REP.
SLOVAKIA
AUSTRIA
HUNGARY
SLOVENIA
ROMANIA
MOLDOVA

MONACO
ITALY
CROATIA
B-H SERBIA MON.
BULGARIA

Bulgarian Orthodoxy *Christianity*

ANDORRA
HOLY SEE
ALB.
MACEDONIA

PORTUGAL
SPAIN

Roman Catholicism

Church of Greece *Christianity*

GREECE

GIBRALTAR

GEORGIA

TURKEY

TUNISIA

Islam

MALTA

CYPRUS

Roman Catholicism

MOROCCO

Islam

Islam
ALGERIA

Islam

LIBYA

EGYPT

see Midd. inse below

CANADA

GREENLAND

Islam
WESTERN SAHARA

Islam
MAURITANIA

CAPE VERDE

MALI
NIGER
CHAD
SUDAN

Islam

U S A

SENEGAL
GAMBIA
GUINEA-BISSAU
GUINEA
SIERRA LEONE
LIBERIA

BURKINA FASO

NIGERIA

CENTRAL AFRICAN REPUBLIC

ETHIOPIA

BERMUDA

CÔTE D'IVOIRE
GHANA
TOGO
BENIN

CAMEROON

DEM. REP. OF CONGO

UGANDA
KENYA

MEXICO

CUBA
BAHAMAS

DOMINICAN REP.
JAMAICA
HAITI
PUERTO RICO

EQUATORIAL GUINEA
SAO TOME & PRINCIPE
GABON
CONGO

RWANDA
BURUNDI
TANZANIA

Roman Catholicism
GUATEMALA
EL SALVADOR
BELIZE
HONDURAS
NICARAGUA

GUADELOUPE
MARTINIQUE
GRENADA
BARBADOS
N. ANTILLES
TRINIDAD & TOBAGO

Roman Catholicism Protestantism Islam

ANGOLA

ZAMBIA
MALAWI
MADA

Roman Catholicism
COSTA RICA
PANAMA

VENEZUELA
GUYANA
SURINAME
FRENCH GUIANA

ZIMBABWE

MOZAMBIQUE

COLOMBIA

NAMIBIA
BOTSWANA

ECUADOR

SWAZILAND

PERU

B R A Z I L

SOUTH AFRICA
LESOTHO

Roman Catholicism
BOLIVIA

Roman Catholicism
CHILE
PARAGUAY

Roman Catholicism
URUGUAY
ARGENTINA

Islamic law
Legal system in Muslim majority states
2006

Islamic law only, based on Shari'ah

combination of Islamic and secular law

Islamic law and secular law exist side by side

secular law only

KAZAKHSTAN

UZBEKISTAN
TURKMENISTAN
TAJIKISTAN
AFGHANISTAN

ALBANIA
TURKEY
SYRIA
IRAQ
IRAN

MOROCCO
TUNISIA
JORDAN
KUWAIT
BAHRAIN
QATAR
UAE
OMAN

PAKISTAN

ALGERIA
LIBYA
EGYPT
SAUDI ARABIA

WESTERN SAHARA

BANGLADESH

MAURITANIA
MALI
NIGER
CHAD
SUDAN
YEMEN
DJIBOUTI

SENEGAL
GAMBIA

NIGERIA

BRUNEI

MALAYSIA

SOMALIA
MALDIVES

INDONESIA

COMOROS

Religious Freedom

China, a legally atheist state, claims to have identified the next Panchen Lama who, in Tibetan Buddhist tradition, has the task of identifying the next Dalai Lama.

State attitudes to religion
2006 or latest available data

- discriminates against all religions and interferes with religious freedom
- favours religion of majority and interferes with or limits freedom of other religions
- favours religion of majority but tolerates other religions
- tolerates all religions

- state declared atheist in law
- state religion established in law
- state recognizes more than one religion or religious group
- monarch must be of given religion
- head of state or government must be of given religion

The connection between politics and religion is evident everywhere, for faith is often a question of government policy and even the cornerstone of the state. Nearly a quarter of the world's states have formal links to a religion but what that means varies markedly. The establishment of an official religion can mean religious intolerance and persecution, but has also proven to be compatible with a secular state and religious tolerance. Religious freedom has increased since the end of the Cold War as the number of states intolerant of all religions has declined.

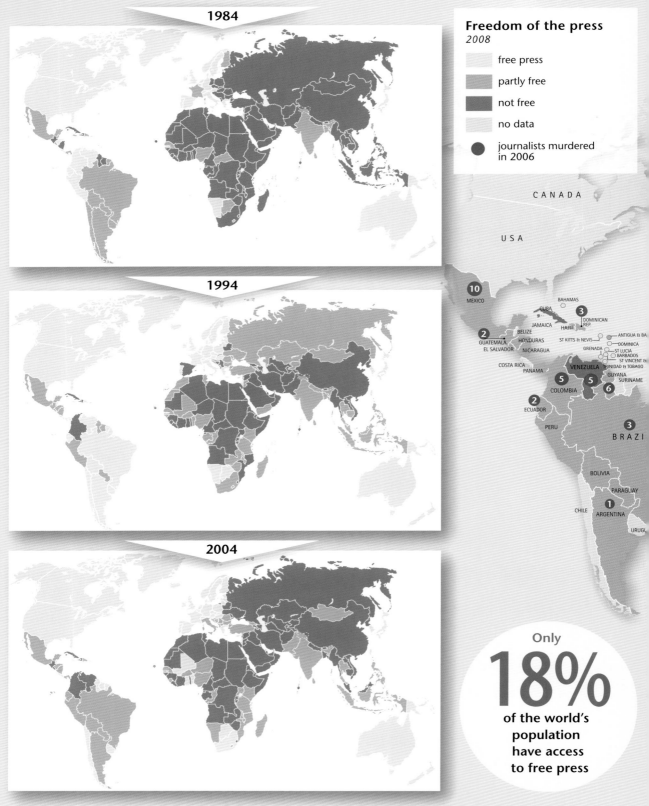

1984

1994

2004

Freedom of the press
2008

free press

partly free

not free

no data

journalists murdered in 2006

CANADA

USA

10
MEXICO

BAHAMAS

CUBA

3
DOMINICAN REP.

JAMAICA

HAITI

BELIZE

GUATEMALA

EL SALVADOR

HONDURAS

NICARAGUA

2

ST KITTS & NEVIS

ANTIGUA & BA

DOMINICA

GRENADA

ST LUCIA

BARBADOS

ST VINCENT &

VENEZUELA

TRINIDAD & TOBAGO

COSTA RICA

PANAMA

5
COLOMBIA

5

6

GUYANA

SURINAME

2
ECUADOR

PERU

3
BRAZI

BOLIVIA

PARAGUAY

1

CHILE

ARGENTINA

URUGU

Only

18%

of the world's
population
have access
to free press

82

Press Freedom

Freedom of the press and news media is an essential element of a free society. Nowhere is the press perfectly free, and arguably nor should it be: most liberal societies agree that hate speech should be restricted. But when information and opinion critical of the state cannot be published, citizens' freedom is at risk.

After a period of improvement in world press freedom in the early 1990s, the next decade saw a steady decline.

In many countries, measures to shackle the press are backed by attacks on journalists. Sometimes servants of the state carry out or tacitly condone the attacks.

Press freedom
Percentage of people living under different degrees of press freedom
2006

free press 18%

not free 42%

partly free 40%

Total population of countries surveyed: 6.5 billion

The worse the human rights situation, the less possible it is to report all or even most abuses. Awareness of the issue is high, but extreme abuses of human rights continue. Although the International Criminal Court is now well established, many perpetrators of human rights abuses clearly count on impunity, and are only slowly being disabused of that notion. Extra-judicial execution is aimed against political opponents, prisoners of war and people regarded as socially undesirable.

2001–08
Guantanamo
The USA has detained 775 people without warrant. About 425 have been released without charge or transferred to native countries. About 270 remained in May 2008.

Executions

Countries with highest number of reported executions
2007

Total known executions: 1,252

Number of people known to be awaiting execution: 27,500

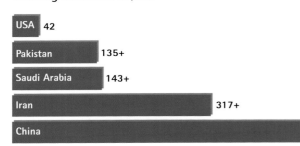

USA 42

Pakistan 135+

Saudi Arabia 143+

Iran 317+

China 470+

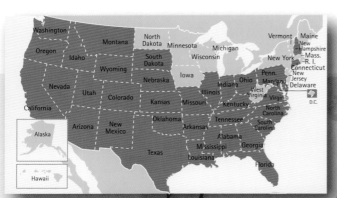

Judicial killings

Status of death penalty
2007

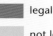

legal

not legal

The number of countries where the death penalty is legal is gradually decreasing.

Human Rights Abuses

Extreme abuse of human rights
2007

Credible reports of:

- extra-judicial executions and enforced disappearances
- torture
- arbitrary arrest and detention
- mistreatment by police and/or prison authorities
- violent and/or abusive treatment of refugees, asylum seekers or immigrants
- other states

Extraordinary rendition
Countries involved in US operations
1995–2008

- suspected terrorists kidnapped in these countries
- transported via these countries
- detained, interrogated and allegedly tortured in these countries

Poverty, sexual and physical abuse, family breakdown, teenage pregnancy, homelessness, drug use and a lack of any alternatives, all put a child at risk of being trafficked. Traffickers promise employment in restaurants, hotels and homes but deliver children into all forms of exploitation. Victims often remain silent rather than risk deportation or institutionalization.

Trafficking can be linked to demand created by tourists and travellers. People who travel to sexually exploit children generally live in industrialized countries but exploit the underage poor in developing countries. However, this form of exploitation takes place within national borders all over the world.

Mexico
Over 16,000 children work as prostitutes, mostly in tourist destinations.

Eastern Europe
Girls as young as 13 are trafficked for sexual exploitation.

Trafficking

Origins and destinations in Europe and Africa
2008 or latest available data

- country of origin
- country of destination
- country of origin and destination
- no data

Trafficking exists within many countries as well as across borders.

Caribbean trafficking routes *2008*

Guatemala Between 1,000 and 1,500 babies and children are sold or trafficked each year for adoption in North America and Europe.

Brazil
Travel agencies or hotels facilitating child sex tourism risk being fined or losing their licence; perpetrators face 10 years imprisonment.

Copyright © Myriad Editions Limited

Trafficking and Sex Tourism

Copyright © Myriad Editions Limited

UK
Paedophiles can be banned from destinations where they could be a risk to children.

Lithuania
Maybe half of all prostitutes are minors. Ten-year-olds from children's homes have been used to make pornographic movies.

In many countries, men prey on under-age and vulnerable girls, often persuading them to steal, smuggle drugs, launder money and obtain loans in addition to working as prostitutes.

Japan
Penalty for sexually exploiting children: 5 years in prison; organizing child sex tours and displaying child pornography: 3 years.

Thailand
Penalty for commercial sexual exploitation of a child: up to 6 years in prison; selling a child for sexual exploitation: up to 20 years.

Cambodia
Over 30% of sex workers in the Mekong region are between 12 and 17 years old.

Map labels (Europe inset)
ICELAND, NORWAY, SWEDEN, FINLAND, ESTONIA, LATVIA, LITHUANIA, UK, IRELAND, DENMARK, NETH, BELGIUM, LUXEMBOURG, GERMANY, POLAND, UKRAINE, FRANCE, AUSTRIA, SLOVAKIA, SLOVENIA, ROMANIA, CROATIA, B-H, SERBIA, BULGARIA, L-MACEDONIA, PORTUGAL, SPAIN, ANDORRA, SWITZ, ITALY, TURKEY

Map labels (main map)
MOROCCO, TUNISIA, ALGERIA, LIBYA, EGYPT, CYPRUS, LEB, SYRIA, GEORGIA, ARMENIA, AZERBAIJAN, TURKMENISTAN, TAJIKISTAN, AFGHANISTAN, KYRGYZSTAN, KAZAKHSTAN, MONGOLIA, CHINA, SOUTH KOREA, JAPAN, TAIWAN, CAPE VERDE, SENEGAL, MALI, NIGER, CHAD, SUDAN, ERITREA, YEMEN, DJIBOUTI, ETHIOPIA, KUWAIT, BAHRAIN, QATAR, OMAN, NEPAL, INDIA, BANGLADESH, LAOS, THAILAND, VIETNAM, CAMBODIA, PHILIPPINES, SIERRA LEONE, BURKINA FASO, TOGO, BENIN, EQUATORIAL GUINEA, DEMOCRATIC REPUBLIC OF CONGO, UGANDA, RWANDA, TANZANIA, SRI LANKA, MALDIVES, ANGOLA, NAMIBIA, BOTSWANA, ZAMBIA, MADAGASCAR, MOZAMBIQUE, SOUTH AFRICA, LESOTHO, AUSTRALIA, NEW ZEALAND

Over 1.2 million children are trafficked every year

South Africa
Prohibits the use of children under 18, for prostitution, pornography, sex trafficking or any other commercial exploitation.

Travelling Sex Offenders
Reported countries of origin and destination *2008*

- country of origin
- country of destination
- no data

- extra-territorial legislation allows prosecution of child sex offender locally or at home
- in addition, special laws forbid travelling with the intent of abusing children

Australia
Penalty for facilitating travel in order to sexually exploit a child: 17 years in prison.

New Zealand
Penalty for facilitating child sex tourism: 7 years in prison. Sex offenders abroad face same sentence as those at home.

Children not in school

Percentage of school-age children
not attending school
by region and economic group
2005

🏃 1 million children
in school

🏃 1 million children
not in school

World total **18%**

Latin America
6%

Middle East and North Africa
19%

West and Central Africa
45%

Eastern and Southern Africa
39%

Where children are working

Regional distribution of
economically active children
aged 5 – 14 years
2004

Latin America
and Caribbean
3%

other
7%

Sub-Saharan
Africa
26%

Asia and
Pacific
64%

The exclusion of the
very poor from the
benefits and rights that
citizens should have
according to international
law begins in many countries
with the non-registration of
births. Left to one side by the
state at the start of their lives,
these children miss out on
health care and education and
head towards a life on the
margins of society, often being
exploited as child labourers.

Birth registration

Percentage of children
registered before
the age of 5 years
2004 or latest available data

- 10% or fewer
- 20% – 39%
- 40% – 59%
- 60% – 79%
- 80% or more
- no data

Children's Rights

South Asia

East Asia and Pacific

Central and Eastern Europe/CIS

Industrialized countries

26%

6%

12%

4%

MONGOLIA

LDOVA

GEORGIA

UZBEKISTAN

ARMENIA AZERBAIJAN

TAJIKISTAN

IRAQ

NORTH KOREA

LESTINE THORITY

NEPAL

SUDAN

INDIA

BANGLADESH

BURMA

LAOS

CAMBODIA VIETNAM

PHILIPPINES

Although the number of children working appears to be declining, around 1 in 5 children are still involved in some form of economic activity, and of these nearly half are involved in hazardous work.

UGANDA

KENYA

RWANDA

BURUNDI

TANZANIA

COMOROS

MBIA

MADAGASCAR

MBABWE

SWAZILAND

LESOTHO

MALDIVES

INDONESIA

EAST TIMOR

21%

10 – 14 years

11%

5 – 9 years

35%

15 – 17 years

Children at work
Economically active children as percentage of age-group
2004

89

Recent economic improvements in many countries have still left women in a much worse position than men – and in some countries the position of women has declined since the early 1990s. Women are, in general, given less well-paid jobs than men, and get paid less than men even when doing the same job. Likewise, although women are participating more in politics than before, most political leaders are men.

Equal rights

Score on the Gender-related Development Index (GDI) *2005*

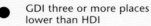

■	below 500 *least equal*
■	500 – 699
	700 – 799
	800 – 899
	900 and above *most equal*
	no data

GDI rank compared with Human Development Index (HDI)

● GDI three or more places lower than HDI

○ GDI three or more places higher than HDI

The Gender Development Index (GDI) compares the life expectancy, literacy, school enrolment, and earned income of men and women within a country. The lower the GDI score, the worse the gender equality.

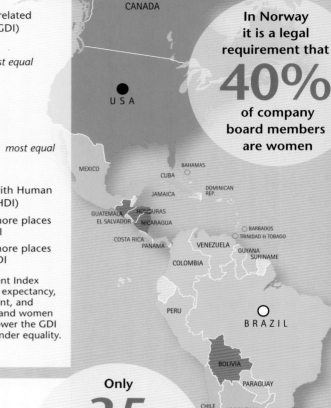

In Norway it is a legal requirement that

40%

of company board members are women

Only

35

countries have ever had a woman head of government

National parliament

Proportion of seats held by women *2006*

■ none	21% – 30%
1% – 10%	more than 30%
11% – 20%	no data

Spain
In April 2008, 50% of the cabinet were women.

Women's Rights

RUSSIA

ICELAND
NORWAY
FINLAND
SWEDEN
ESTONIA
LATVIA
DENMARK
IRELAND UK RUSSIA LITHUANIA
NETH. BELARUS
GERMANY POLAND
BEL. UKRAINE
LUX. CZ. REP. SL.
SWITZ. NDS. HUN. MOLDOVA
FRANCE ITALY CRO. ROM.
AUS. BUL.
ALB. MAC.
SPAIN GREECE TURKEY
PORTUGAL MALTA CYPRUS SYRIA
TUNISIA LEB.
MOROCCO ISRAEL JORDAN

KAZAKHSTAN
MONGOLIA
UZBEKISTAN KYRGYZSTAN
AZERBAIJAN TAJIKISTAN
ARMENIA
IRAN CHINA
KUWAIT PAKISTAN NEPAL
BAHRAIN SOUTH KOREA JAPAN
QATAR INDIA BANGLADESH
UAE Hong Kong SAR
SAUDI ARABIA OMAN LAOS

ALGERIA LIBYA
AURITANIA MALI NIGER CHAD SUDAN ERITREA YEMEN DJIBOUTI
GAMBIA BURKINA FASO NIGERIA ETHIOPIA
GUINEA-BISSAU BENIN CENTRAL AFRICAN REPUBLIC UGANDA
SIERRA LEONE CÔTE D'IVOIRE GHANA TOGO CAMEROON KENYA
EQUATORIAL GUINEA DEMOCRATIC REPUBLIC OF CONGO RWANDA
SAO TOME & PRINCIPE GABON CONGO BURUNDI TANZANIA
COMOROS
ANGOLA MALAWI MADAGASCAR MAURITIUS
ZAMBIA ZIMBABWE MOZAMBIQUE
NAMIBIA BOTSWANA SWAZILAND
SOUTH AFRICA LESOTHO

THAILAND VIETNAM CAMBODIA
SRI LANKA MALAYSIA BRUNEI
MALDIVES PHILIPPINES SAMOA FIJI TONGA
INDONESIA PAPUA NEW GUINEA

AUSTRALIA
NEW ZEALAND

Even though many male politicians are reviled, most images of good leadership evoke demeanour and attitudes associated with masculinity.

Women earners
The number of women involved in economic activity for every 100 men
2005

	100%	34%	44%	65%	72%	73%	79%	79%
	men	Arab States	South Asia	Latin America & Caribbean	OECD countries	Sub-Saharan Africa	East Asia and Pacific	Eastern Europe, Russia and Central Asia

USA
Same-sex couples may jointly petition for the right to adopt in at least 16 states.

GREENLAND

ICELAND

NORWAY

SWED

UK   DENMARK

NETH.

BELA

CZ.
REP.

BELGIUM

LUX.
FRANCE   SWITZ.

AUS.
SL
CRO.

ANDORRA

SPAIN

GRE

TUNISIA

MOROCCO

ALGERIA

LIB

C A N A D A

Washington

Oregon

California

U S A

NH
VT ME
MA
CT
NJ

MEXICO

BELIZE

JAMAICA

NICARAGUA

ST KITTS & NEVIS

GRENADA

DOMINICA
ST LUCIA
BARBADOS
TRINIDAD & TOBAGO

GUYANA

MAURITANIA

SENEGAL
GAMBIA

GUINEA

SIERRA LEONE

LIBERIA

GHANA
TOGO
BENIN

NIGERIA

CAMEROON

Legislation on homosexuality
2007

Legal status of union between same-sex couples:

- marriage allowed
- civil unions allowed
- common-law marriage recognized

Penalties imposed for same-sex private consensual sex:

- death penalty
- prison sentence over 10 years
- prison sentence under 10 years
- no legal status for same-sex unions and private same-sex acts not penalized

- joint adoption by same-sex couples allowed
- open homosexuals prohibited from serving in army

B R A Z I L

ANGO

NAMIBI

BOTSWANA

ARGENTINA

Northern Nigeria
12 states have adopted laws under which the maximum penalty for male homosexuals is death.

Gay Rights

There are some countries where the right for people to make their own sexual preference is recognized, and freedom in this domain has expanded markedly in recent times. But there remain political parties and governments that are committed to allowing only a narrow range of sexual activity. Those whose sexual preference takes them outside the norm – especially gay men – face pressures that are subtle and social when they are not open and political.

Russia
Homosexuality was decriminalized in 1993, but there are increasingly strong political threats to re-criminalize it.

Civil partnerships in the UK give same-sex couples equal legal rights to those of married heterosexual couples. They were introduced in December 2005.

Zanzibar, Tanzania
Gay sex outlawed in 2004, with prison terms of up to 25 years.

Aceh, Indonesia
Although same-sex acts are legal in Indonesia, they are banned for Muslims in Aceh province.

Australia
Same-sex couples have been allowed to adopt in Western Australia since 2002, and in the Australian Capital Territory since 2004.

RUSSIA

CHECHNYA

UZBEKISTAN

TURKMENISTAN

CYPRUS
SYRIA
LEB.
ISRAEL

AFGHANISTAN

IRAN

PAKISTAN

NEPAL

BHUTAN

BAHRAIN
QATAR
UAE

SAUDI ARABIA

OMAN

INDIA

BANGLADESH

BURMA

JDAN

ERITREA
YEMEN
DJIBOUTI

ETHIOPIA

SRI LANKA

UGANDA
KENYA
SOMALIA

RWANDA
BURUNDI

TANZANIA   Zanzibar

BIA
MALAWI

3ABWE

MOZAMBIQUE

SWAZILAND

BRUNEI

MALAYSIA

SINGAPORE

INDONESIA

PAPUA NEW GUINEA

AUSTRALIA

NEW ZEALAND

MARSHALL ISLANDS

NAURU   KIRIBATI

SOLOMON ISLANDS

TUVALU

TOKELAU

SAMOA

FIJI

COOK ISLANDS

TONGA   NIUE

PALAU

93

Fighter graffiti on a hospital wall in eastern Chad.
The area is destabilized by refugees and militia from
the crisis in neighbouring Darfur, Sudan.

Undernourished people
As percentage of population
2002–04

- 40% or more
- 20% – 39%
- 10% – 19%
- 3% – 9%
- fewer than 2.5%
- non-recipients of aid or no data

vitamin A deficiency affects 40% or more pre-school children and women of child-bearing age *risk of blindness*

iodine deficiency affects 40% or more of population *risk of reduced mental capacity*

food aid: over 40 million tonnes committed by World Food Programme 2007–08

CANADA

USA

ICELAND

NORWAY

SWED

UK   DENMARK
IRELAND   RU
          NETH.   GERMANY
          BEL.   CZ.
          LUX.   REP.
FRANCE   SW.   AUS.
          SLOVENIA CRO.

PORTUGAL   SPAIN
                              ITALY

                    TUNISIA
MOROCCO   MA

          ALGERIA   LIE

MEXICO

BAHAMAS
CUBA
JAMAICA
          DOMINICAN
          REP.
          HAITI

BELIZE
GUATEMALA   HONDURAS
EL SALVADOR NICARAGUA
             ST VINCENT & GRENADINES
COSTA RICA   GRENADA
PANAMA

—ST KITTS & NEVIS
—DOMINICA
—ST LUCIA
—BARBADOS
—TRINIDAD & TOBAGO

VENEZUELA
COLOMBIA
          GUYANA
          SURINAME

ECUADOR

PERU

BRAZIL

BOLIVIA

CHILE   PARAGUAY

ARGENTINA

URUGUAY

MAURITANIA   MALI   NIGER

                    SENEGAL
GAMBIA   BURKINA
          GUINEA-   FASO
          BISSAU GUINEA   NIGERIA
          SIERRA LEONE CÔTE GHANA TOGO BENIN
                        D'IVOIRE
          LIBERIA   CAMEROON

                              GABON
          SAO TOME
          & PRINCIPE   CONGO

                                   ANG

                              NAM

                              BOTSWA

Concern about climate change has highlighted threats to food security, especially in developing countries.

Poor nutrition in babies and children can increase their risk of dying from infectious diseases. Half a million children are blind because their diet is deficient in vitamin A.

Food price rises
Massive increases in grain prices in 2007–08 severely affected poor people and led to food riots around the globe.

RUSSIA

KAZAKHSTAN

MONGOLIA

UZBEKISTAN
KYRGYZSTAN
NORTH KOREA
JAPAN

TURKMENISTAN
TAJIKISTAN
SOUTH KOREA

GEORGIA
AZERBAIJAN
ARMENIA

AFGHANISTAN
CHINA

SYRIA
LEB.
IRAN

JORDAN
KUWAIT

PAKISTAN
NEPAL

UAE

SAUDI ARABIA
INDIA
BANGLADESH
BURMA
LAOS

EGYPT

THAILAND
VIETNAM

ERITREA
YEMEN
PHILIPPINES

SUDAN
DJIBOUTI
CAMBODIA

ETHIOPIA
SRI LANKA
BRUNEI

SOMALIA
MALDIVES
MALAYSIA

UGANDA
KENYA

RWANDA
BURUNDI
SEYCHELLES

INDONESIA

TANZANIA

COMOROS
EAST TIMOR

MALAWI

MADAGASCAR
MAURITIUS

MOZAMBIQUE

AUSTRALIA

SWAZILAND
LESOTHO

MICRONESIA, FED. STATES OF
MARSHALL ISLANDS
KIRIBATI
SOLOMON ISLANDS
SAMOA
VANUATU
FIJI

NEW ZEALAND

Because of poverty the diet of many people is low in calories or deficient in vital micronutrients. Malnourished people can get caught in a vicious cycle, lacking the energy to work or go to school, which would enable them to raise their standard of living and improve their diet.

The escalating price of staple foods causes hardship and hunger among poor people worldwide. In 2008, the World Food Programme warned that it would be unable to purchase sufficient supplies to carry out its work.

USA
19% of children aged 6–11 were obese in 2004.

America's spreading obesity

Percentage of adults who are obese *1996, 2001, 2006*

- ■ 25% or more
- ▨ 20% – 24%
- ▨ 15% – 19%
- ▨ 10% – 14%
- ▨ no data

Obesity

England
14% of children aged 2–10 were obese in 2003.

Overweight adults
Percentage of people aged 15–100 years with BMI over 25
2005

- 70% or more
- 50% – 69%
- 25% – 49%
- 10% – 24%
- fewer than 10%
- no data

Australia
7% of children were obese in 2006.

Body Mass Index (BMI) assesses weight in relation to height. A BMI score equals a person's weight (in kg) divided by their height (in metres) squared.

BMI score under 18.5: underweight
  18.5 – 24.9: healthy
  25.0 – 29.9: overweight
  over 30.0: obese

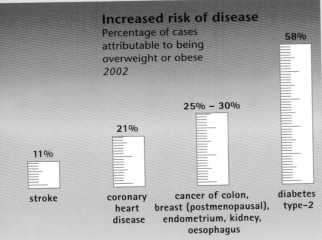

Increased risk of disease
Percentage of cases attributable to being overweight or obese
2002

- stroke — 11%
- coronary heart disease — 21%
- cancer of colon, breast (postmenopausal), endometrium, kidney, oesophagus — 25% – 30%
- diabetes type-2 — 58%

Worldwide, people are eating more meat, dairy products and sugary foods, and their weight is increasing as a consequence. Even in countries where the majority of people are undernourished, those who can afford it are over-eating, their extra flesh often seen as a prestigious indication of their wealth. In rich countries, cheap processed foods are high in animal fats and sugars, so a poor diet is more likely to lead to weight gain. Obesity leads to an increased risk of several serious diseases. The likely consequences are serious, not only for the individuals concerned but for society as a whole as health services struggle to cope with the increased strain.

A cigarette is the only legal consumer product that kills through normal use. And the full health and economic impacts of the increasing popularity of cigarettes over the last 50 years are yet to be felt. Half of the 650 million people who currently smoke will eventually be killed by the habit.

With advertising controls being tightened in industrialized countries, tobacco companies are increasingly seeking to expand into developing countries in an effort to maintain sales.

The number of young smokers around the world is increasing, with 25% of them trying their first cigarette before the age of ten.

Deaths
Increasing deaths due to tobacco
1950–2030 projected

—— industrialized countries

—— developing countries

7 million *projected*

3 million *projected*

2.1 million

2.1 million

1.3 million

0.3 million

0.2 million

1950   1975   2000   2025–30

Global cigarette consumption
Total number of cigarettes
smoked each year
1930–2002
billions

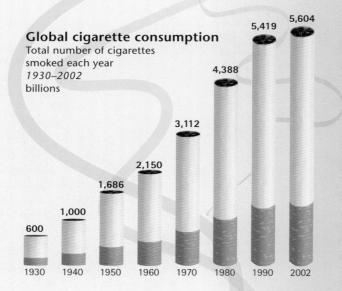

600   1,000   1,686   2,150   3,112   4,388   5,419   5,604

1930   1940   1950   1960   1970   1980   1990   2002

Tobacco causes

10%

of adult deaths worldwide

India
If present trends continue, by 2010 tobacco will kill 1 million men aged 25 to 69 years every year.

men

Smoking among adults
Percentage who smoke cigarettes
2005 or latest available data

- 60% or more
- 50% – 59.9%
- 40% – 49.9%
- 30% – 39.9%
- 20% – 29.9%
- fewer than 20%
- no data

women

Although fewer women smoke than men, there is a worrying increase among younger women in many countries.

In 2002, there were 10.9 million new cancer cases in the world, and 6.7 million deaths. The most common cancers worldwide are lung, breast, large intestine (colon and rectum), stomach and prostate. Liver cancer is the most common cancer for men in several African countries, although Kaposi sarcoma has become the most common in those countries severely affected by the AIDS epidemic.

The risk of getting cancer is higher in the industrialized world, but in the developing world lack of treatment means that it is more likely to be fatal.

Sex differences
New cancer cases by sex 2002 thousands

♂ male | female ♀

	male		female	
lung	965		387	
breast (female)			1,151	
colon and rectum	550		473	
stomach	603		331	
prostate	679			
liver	442		184	
cervix and uterus			493	
oesophagus	315		147	
bladder	274		83	
ovary			204	
leukaemia	171		129	
non-Hodgkin lymphoma	175		125	
oral cavity	176		98	
pancreas	125		107	
kidney	129		79	

Differences around the world
New cancer cases in industrialized and developing countries *2002* thousands

- industrialized countries
- developing countries

46% of new cancer cases occur in industrialized countries, home to **19%** of the world's population

	industrialized	developing
lung	677	672
colon and rectum	666	356
breast	636	514
prostate	513	165
stomach	311	619
bladder	225	131
non-Hodgkin lymphoma	151	149
kidney	140	68
pancreas	135	97
leukaemia	124	176
liver	110	513
ovary	97	108
oral cavity	91	183
cervix uteri	83	409
oesophagus	74	386

Cancer

The most common cancers
Cases by type of cancer *2002*

- bladder
- breast
- cervix
- colon and rectum
- Kaposi sarcoma
- liver
- lung
- non-Hodgkin lymphoma
- oesophagus
- oral cavity
- prostate
- stomach
- no data

men

women

Copyright © Myriad Editions Limited

Every day during 2007 over 6,800 people became infected with HIV, and over 5,700 people died from AIDS, mostly because of inadequate access to HIV prevention and treatment services. Sub-Saharan Africa is the worst-affected region, with widespread infection having a devastating social and economic impact.

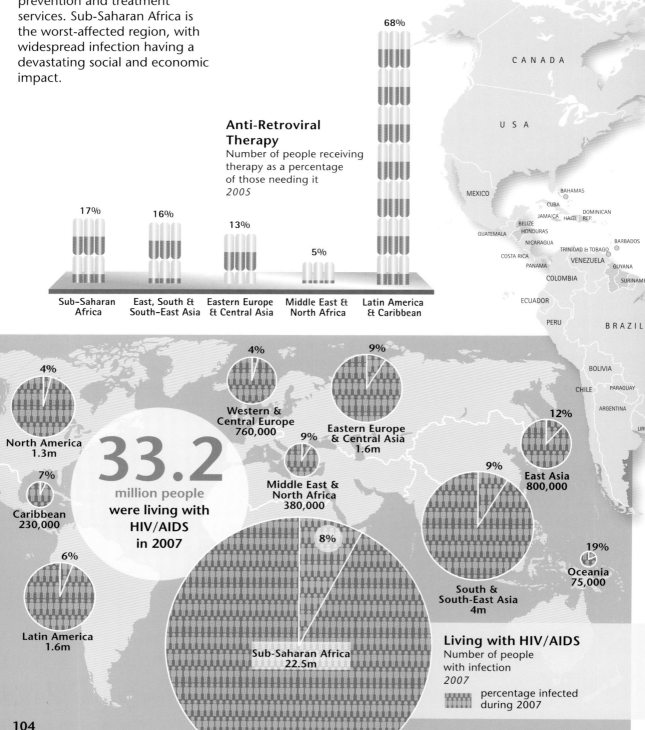

Anti-Retroviral Therapy
Number of people receiving therapy as a percentage of those needing it
2005

68%

17%
Sub-Saharan Africa

16%
East, South & South-East Asia

13%
Eastern Europe & Central Asia

5%
Middle East & North Africa

Latin America & Caribbean

CANADA

USA

MEXICO

BAHAMAS
CUBA
JAMAICA   HAITI   DOMINICAN REP.
BELIZE
GUATEMALA   HONDURAS
NICARAGUA   TRINIDAD & TOBAGO   BARBADOS
COSTA RICA   VENEZUELA   GUYANA
PANAMA   SURINAME
COLOMBIA
ECUADOR
PERU   BRAZIL
BOLIVIA
CHILE   PARAGUAY
ARGENTINA   URU

4%
North America
1.3m

7%
Caribbean
230,000

6%
Latin America
1.6m

33.2
million people
were living with
HIV/AIDS
in 2007

4%
Western & Central Europe
760,000

9%
Middle East & North Africa
380,000

9%
Eastern Europe & Central Asia
1.6m

8%
Sub-Saharan Africa
22.5m

9%
South & South-East Asia
4m

12%
East Asia
800,000

19%
Oceania
75,000

Living with HIV/AIDS
Number of people with infection
2007

percentage infected during 2007

104

HIV/AIDS

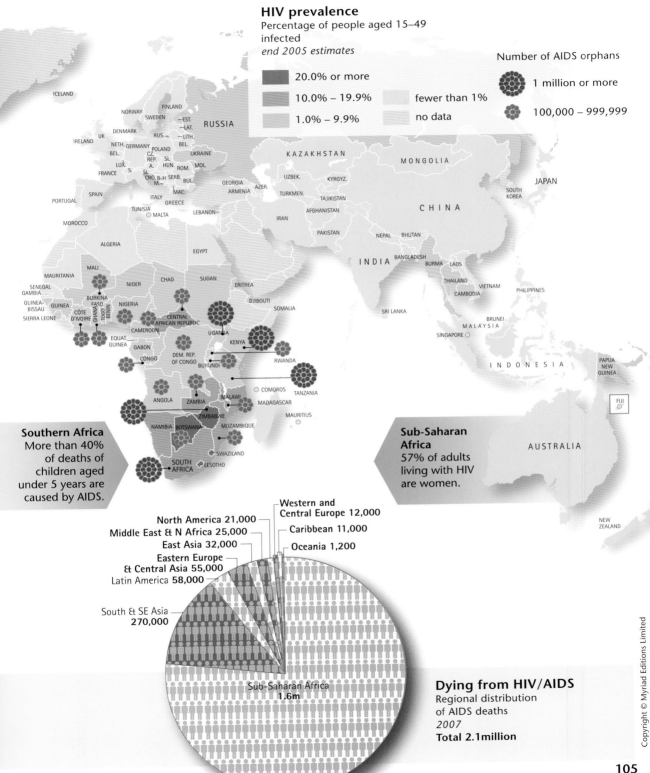

HIV prevalence
Percentage of people aged 15–49
infected
end 2005 estimates

- 20.0% or more
- 10.0% – 19.9%
- 1.0% – 9.9%
- fewer than 1%
- no data

Number of AIDS orphans
- 1 million or more
- 100,000 – 999,999

Southern Africa
More than 40% of deaths of children aged under 5 years are caused by AIDS.

Sub-Saharan Africa
57% of adults living with HIV are women.

Dying from HIV/AIDS
Regional distribution of AIDS deaths
2007
Total 2.1million

- Western and Central Europe 12,000
- North America 21,000
- Middle East & N Africa 25,000
- Caribbean 11,000
- East Asia 32,000
- Eastern Europe & Central Asia 55,000
- Oceania 1,200
- Latin America 58,000
- South & SE Asia 270,000
- Sub-Saharan Africa 1.6m

Women and children search for edible roots in a river bed during the dry season in Burkina Faso. Conditions are made worse by over-grazing, infestations, and changes in weather due to climate change.

The **Panamanian golden frog** is one of many amphibians threatened by the chytrid fungus that has swept through Central America. Scientists have removed the remaining individuals from the wild in an attempt to save them.

Protected areas
Percentage of land under World Conservation Union (IUCN) protection *2004*

- 10% or more
- 5% – 9%
- less than 5%
- no data

Biodiversity

1,094
mammal species were considered threatened in 2007

Since the start of the industrial age, humankind has made ever-increasing demands on the environment to satisfy our need for water, fuel and food. In so doing, we threaten the survival of other species. Most governments are taking steps to protect a proportion of the natural habitat, but these pockets of land may not be enough to protect biodiversity.

MONGOLIA

CHINA

NORTH KOREA

SOUTH KOREA

JAPAN

NEPAL

BHUTAN

BANGLADESH

BURMA

LAOS

Hong Kong SAR

TAIWAN

THAILAND

VIETNAM

CAMBODIA

PHILIPPINES

SRI LANKA

BRUNEI

MALAYSIA

SINGAPORE

INDONESIA

PALAU

PAPUA NEW GUINEA

SOLOMON ISLANDS

AUSTRALIA

NEW CALEDONIA

NEW ZEALAND

Mammals
Number of species threatened
2006

- 146
- 50 – 99
- 25 – 49
- 10 – 24
- fewer than 10
- no data

more than 50 bird species threatened 2006

more than 200 plant species threatened

Threatened species
Species assessed as threatened as percentage of those evaluated by IUCN
2007

birds 12%

mammals 22%

reptiles 30%

amphibians 31%

fishes 39%

invertebrates 51%

plants 70%

Rainforest loss
1990–2005

square kilometres lost

area lost as percentage of total rainforest in region

Region	Percentage lost	Square kilometres lost
Thailand	9%	14,450
Malaysia	7%	14,860
Cameroon	13%	33,000
Philippines	32%	34,120
Congo, D.R.	5%	69,210
Burma	18%	69,970
Indonesia	24%	280,720
Brazil	8%	423,290

One in four people live in areas with insufficient water to support them. This means that water is being used at an unsustainable level, with rivers running dry, underground aquifers being drained to make up the shortfall, and energy being used to desalinate water. Throughout much of Sub-Saharan Africa, even where water is available, the infrastructure needed to get it to people is absent or poorly maintained. As a result, countries that are comparatively well off in water actually use relatively little. The problem is not the availability of the resource, but a shortfall in the ability to govern its use so as to benefit the majority of people.

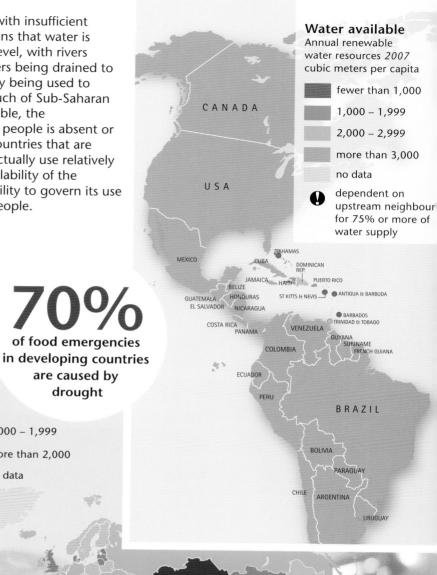

Water available
Annual renewable water resources *2007*
cubic meters per capita

- fewer than 1,000
- 1,000 – 1,999
- 2,000 – 2,999
- more than 3,000
- no data
- ❶ dependent on upstream neighbour for 75% or more of water supply

CANADA
USA
MEXICO
BAHAMAS
CUBA
DOMINICAN REP.
JAMAICA
HAITI
PUERTO RICO
BELIZE
ST KITTS & NEVIS
ANTIGUA & BARBUDA
GUATEMALA
HONDURAS
EL SALVADOR
NICARAGUA
BARBADOS
COSTA RICA
TRINIDAD & TOBAGO
PANAMA
VENEZUELA
GUYANA
SURINAME
COLOMBIA
FRENCH GUIANA
ECUADOR
PERU
BRAZIL
BOLIVIA
PARAGUAY
CHILE
ARGENTINA
URUGUAY

70%
of food emergencies in developing countries are caused by drought

Water used
Amount used each year for industries, agricultural and domestic purposes
2007 or latest available data
cubic meters per capita

- fewer than 250
- 250 – 499
- 500 – 1,000
- 1,000 – 1,999
- more than 2,000
- no data

Water Resources

Rivers that cross several national boundaries, such as the Nile, the Ganges–Brahmaputra system and the Niger offer multiple opportunities for conflict or co-operation.

Regional water use
Percentage of water used by each sector
2008

- agriculture
- industry
- domestic

North America 13% / 39% / 48%

Europe 15% / 32% / 53%

Latin America 19% / 10% / 71%

Africa 4% / 10% / 86%

Asia 7% / 11% / 81%

Oceania 18% / 10% / 72%

Africa
Irrigation markedly boosts crop yields, yet only 4% of African cropland is irrigated.

Water for food
It takes up to 5,000 litres a day to produce a person's food.

Waste is one of the great unspoken problems of our time. It is an issue that reaches from the actions of individuals to the operation of large-scale industry. Non-stop growth in garbage is consuming landfill sites faster than they can be created. Commercial enterprises have stepped in, and recycling rubbish has become a global business worth billions of dollars, yet still the problem mounts. At one end of the scale lie the plastic bags that supermarkets give away for free and that end up in the sea, killing dolphins. At the other end lies industrial pollution and the unresolved problem of disposing of the radioactive waste products of nuclear power.

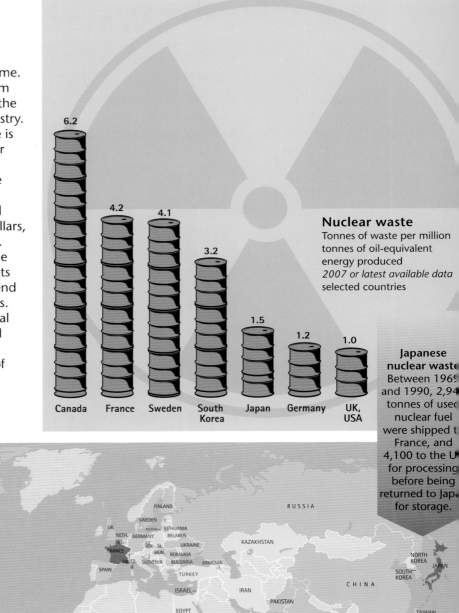

Nuclear waste
Tonnes of waste per million tonnes of oil-equivalent energy produced
2007 or latest available data
selected countries

Canada	6.2
France	4.2
Sweden	4.1
South Korea	3.2
Japan	1.5
Germany	1.2
UK, USA	1.0

Japanese nuclear waste
Between 1969 and 1990, 2,94[?] tonnes of used nuclear fuel were shipped t[?] France, and 4,100 to the U[?] for processing before being returned to Jap[?] for storage.

US nuclear waste
Between 1968 and 2002, over 47,000 tonnes of uranium was processed.

Nuclear power
Jan 2008

operates 50 or more commercial nuclear power stations

operates fewer than 50 commercial nuclear power stations

plans or proposes to operate commercial nuclear power station

CANADA · USA · MEXICO · BRAZIL · ARGENTINA · SOUTH AFRICA
UK · NETH. · BEL. · FRANCE · SPAIN · SWITZ. · GERMANY · CZ. REP. · SL. · HUN. · SLOVENIA · SWEDEN · FINLAND · RUSSIA · LITHUANIA · BELARUS · UKRAINE · ROMANIA · BULGARIA · ARMENIA · TURKEY · ISRAEL · EGYPT · IRAN · PAKISTAN · KAZAKHSTAN · CHINA · INDIA · BANGLADESH · NORTH KOREA · SOUTH KOREA · JAPAN · TAIWAN · VIETNAM · THAILAND · INDONESIA

Waste

Household waste
Municipal waste produced in OECD countries
2007 or latest available data
kg per person

- 650 or more
- 500 – 649
- 250 – 499

action taken or planned in some cities to ban or discourage plastic bags

ocean currents

high density of plastic waste

CANADA

Alaska

Leaf Rapids, Manitoba

Portland, Oregon

Oakland, San Francisco

USA

MEXICO

plastic waste

HAWAII

US waste disposal methods
2008

recycle 31%

landfill 55%

burn 14%

ICELAND NORWAY SWEDEN

FINLAND

UK DENMARK

IRELAND NETH. GER. POLAND

BELGIUM LUX. AUS. CZ. REP.

SWITZ. SLOVAKIA

HUNGARY

PORTUGAL SPAIN

FRANCE ITALY GREECE

TURKEY

ISRAEL

Ladakh Province

New Delhi
INDIA
Mumbai

ERITREA

UGANDA

RWANDA KENYA

TANZANIA
Zanzibar

SOUTH AFRICA

Ireland
Plastic-bag use dropped by 90% after the government introduced a tax on them in 2002.

Flooding
Plastic bags blocking the drains contributed to the floods in Mumbai in 2005.

South Africa
Flimsy plastic bags draped in trees were so ubiquitous that they became known as the "national flower".

One-third of the world's electronics recycling takes place in China, where the demand for the waste product is high, but the pollution created by the recycling is causing intense concern.

Great Pacific Garbage Patch
A 10-metre thick "soup" of plastic flotsam is circulating in areas of the Pacific. An immediate hazard to wildlife, the chemicals it releases will affect human health for centuries to come.

SOUTH KOREA JAPAN

CHINA
BHUTAN TAIWAN

BANGLADESH

plastic waste

HAWAII

AUSTRALIA

Victoria

Tasmania Coles Bay

NEW ZEALAND

Macquarie Island

Southern ocean
A clean-up of the beaches of Macquarie Island in 2004 led to the collection of over 1,000 pieces of rubbish, half of it plastic bottles.

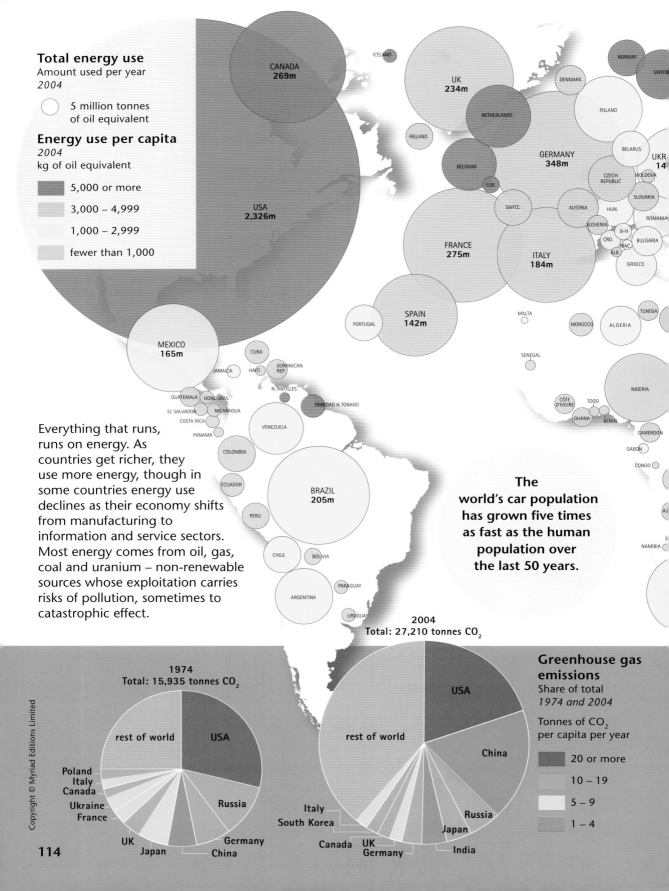

Total energy use
Amount used per year
2004

◯ 5 million tonnes
    of oil equivalent

Energy use per capita
2004
kg of oil equivalent

- 5,000 or more
- 3,000 – 4,999
- 1,000 – 2,999
- fewer than 1,000

ICELAND

NORWAY

SWED

CANADA
269m

UK
234m

DENMARK

POLAND

NETHERLANDS

IRELAND

GERMANY
348m

BELARUS

UKR
14

BELGIUM

LUX.

CZECH
REPUBLIC

MOLDOVA

SLOVAKIA

USA
2,326m

SWITZ.

AUSTRIA

HUN.

ROMANIA

SLOVENIA

B-H

FRANCE
275m

CRO.

MAC.

BULGARIA

ALB.

ITALY
184m

GREECE

SPAIN
142m

MALTA

MOROCCO

ALGERIA

TUNISIA

PORTUGAL

MEXICO
165m

CUBA

SENEGAL

JAMAICA

HAITI

DOMINICAN
REP.

N. ANTILLES

NIGERIA

GUATEMALA

HONDURAS

CÔTE
D'IVOIRE

TOGO

EL SALVADOR

NICARAGUA

TRINIDAD & TOBAGO

GHANA

BENIN

COSTA RICA

CAMEROON

PANAMA

VENEZUELA

GABON

COLOMBIA

CONGO

ECUADOR

BRAZIL
205m

Everything that runs,
runs on energy. As
countries get richer, they
use more energy, though in
some countries energy use
declines as their economy shifts
from manufacturing to
information and service sectors.
Most energy comes from oil, gas,
coal and uranium – non-renewable
sources whose exploitation carries
risks of pollution, sometimes to
catastrophic effect.

PERU

CHILE

BOLIVIA

PARAGUAY

ARGENTINA

URUGUAY

**The
world's car population
has grown five times
as fast as the human
population over
the last 50 years.**

NAMIBIA

2004
Total: 27,210 tonnes CO_2

1974
Total: 15,935 tonnes CO_2

rest of world

USA

Poland
Italy
Canada

Ukraine
France

UK

Japan

Russia

Germany
China

rest of world

USA

China

Italy
South Korea

Canada

UK
Germany

Russia

Japan

India

**Greenhouse gas
emissions**
Share of total
1974 and 2004

Tonnes of CO_2
per capita per year

- 20 or more
- 10 – 19
- 5 – 9
- 1 – 4

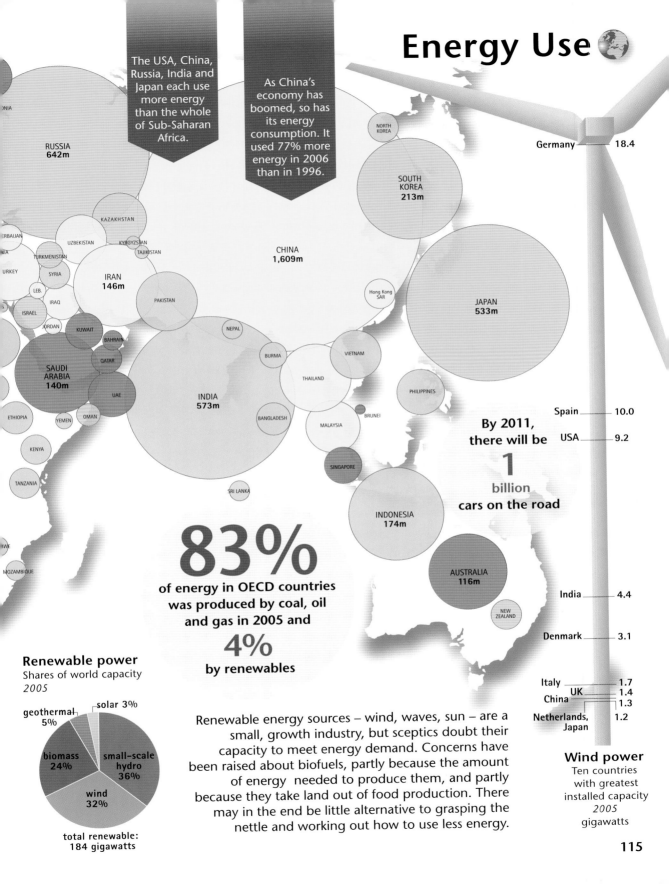

The USA, China, Russia, India and Japan each use more energy than the whole of Sub-Saharan Africa.

As China's economy has boomed, so has its energy consumption. It used 77% more energy in 2006 than in 1996.

NORTH KOREA

SOUTH KOREA
213m

Germany ——— 18.4

RUSSIA
642m

KAZAKHSTAN

CHINA
1,609m

Hong Kong
SAR

JAPAN
533m

ONIA

ERBAIJAN

UZBEKISTAN

KYRGYZSTAN

TAJIKISTAN

TURKMENISTAN

SYRIA

URKEY

LEB.

IRAQ

ISRAEL

JORDAN

KUWAIT

BAHRAIN

QATAR

UAE

IRAN
146m

PAKISTAN

NEPAL

BURMA

VIETNAM

THAILAND

PHILIPPINES

SAUDI
ARABIA
140m

INDIA
573m

BANGLADESH

MALAYSIA

BRUNEI

By 2011, there will be

1

billion
cars on the road

Spain ——— 10.0

USA ——— 9.2

ETHIOPIA

YEMEN

OMAN

KENYA

TANZANIA

SRI LANKA

SINGAPORE

SWE

MOZAMBIQUE

INDONESIA
174m

AUSTRALIA
116m

NEW
ZEALAND

India ——— 4.4

Denmark ——— 3.1

83%

of energy in OECD countries was produced by coal, oil and gas in 2005 and

4%
by renewables

Italy ——— 1.7
UK ——— 1.4
China ——— 1.3
Netherlands, ——— 1.2
Japan

Renewable power
Shares of world capacity
2005

- solar 3%
- geothermal 5%
- biomass 24%
- small–scale hydro 36%
- wind 32%

total renewable:
184 gigawatts

Wind power
Ten countries with greatest installed capacity
2005
gigawatts

Renewable energy sources – wind, waves, sun – are a small, growth industry, but sceptics doubt their capacity to meet energy demand. Concerns have been raised about biofuels, partly because the amount of energy needed to produce them, and partly because they take land out of food production. There may in the end be little alternative to grasping the nettle and working out how to use less energy.

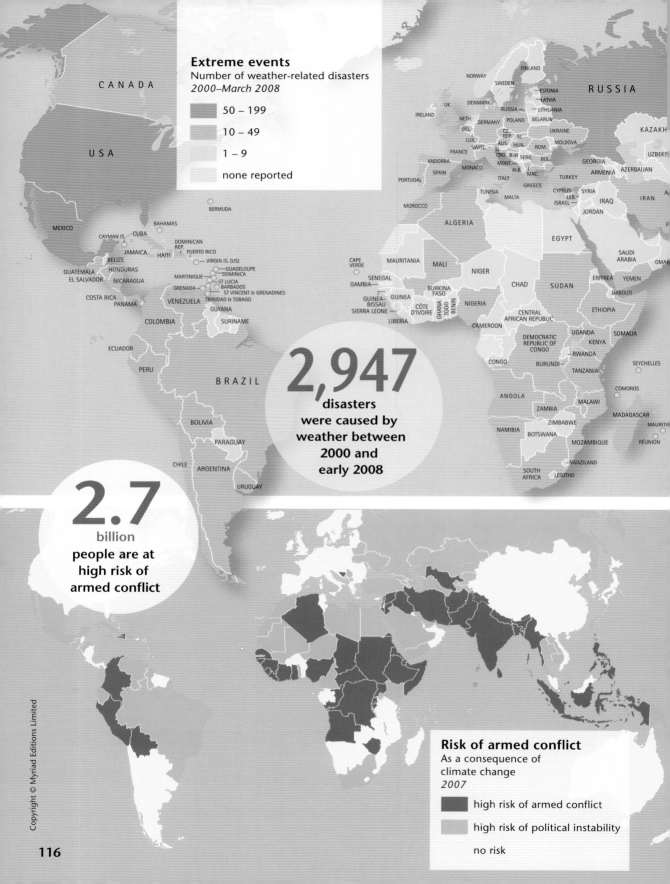

Extreme events
Number of weather-related disasters
2000–March 2008

50 – 199

10 – 49

1 – 9

none reported

CANADA

USA

BERMUDA

MEXICO

BAHAMAS

CAYMAN IS. CUBA

JAMAICA HAITI

DOMINICAN REP. PUERTO RICO

VIRGIN IS. (US)

GUADELOUPE
DOMINICA
MARTINIQUE
ST LUCIA
BARBADOS
ST VINCENT & GRENADINES
TRINIDAD & TOBAGO

BELIZE
GUATEMALA
EL SALVADOR HONDURAS
NICARAGUA

GRENADA

COSTA RICA
PANAMA

VENEZUELA

GUYANA

COLOMBIA

SURINAME

ECUADOR

PERU

BRAZIL

BOLIVIA

PARAGUAY

CHILE ARGENTINA

URUGUAY

NORWAY
SWEDEN
FINLAND

DENMARK
ESTONIA
LATVIA
LITHUANIA

IRELAND

UK

NETH.
BEL.
LUX.

GERMANY POLAND BELARUS

RUSSIA

RUSSIA

UKRAINE

CZ. REP. SL.
AUS. HUN.
SWITZ. SL.
CRO. B-H
MONT. SERB.
ALB. MAC.

MOLDOVA

FRANCE

ANDORRA

PORTUGAL

SPAIN

MONACO

ITALY

ROM.

BUL.

GEORGIA

ARMENIA

AZERBAIJAN

KAZAKH

UZBEKIS

TUNISIA

GREECE

TURKEY

CYPRUS
LEB.
ISRAEL

SYRIA

IRAQ

IRAN

MALTA

MOROCCO

JORDAN

ALGERIA

EGYPT

SAUDI
ARABIA

OMA

CAPE
VERDE

MAURITANIA

MALI

NIGER

CHAD

SUDAN

ERITREA

YEMEN

DJIBOUTI

SENEGAL
GAMBIA
GUINEA-
BISSAU GUINEA
SIERRA LEONE

BURKINA
FASO

CÔTE
D'IVOIRE

GHANA
TOGO BENIN

NIGERIA

LIBERIA

CENTRAL
AFRICAN REPUBLIC

CAMEROON

ETHIOPIA

SOMALIA

CONGO

DEMOCRATIC
REPUBLIC OF
CONGO

UGANDA KENYA

RWANDA
BURUNDI

SEYCHELLES

TANZANIA

ANGOLA

ZAMBIA

MALAWI

COMOROS

MADAGASCAR

MAURITI

NAMIBIA

ZIMBABWE

BOTSWANA

MOZAMBIQUE

RÉUNION

SOUTH
AFRICA

SWAZILAND

LESOTHO

2,947
**disasters
were caused by
weather between
2000 and
early 2008**

2.7
billion
**people are at
high risk of
armed conflict**

Risk of armed conflict
As a consequence of
climate change
2007

high risk of armed conflict

high risk of political instability

no risk

Climate Change

The science of predicting the effects of climate change is still developing. As we learn more, the news tends to get worse. It is widely accepted that higher temperatures will generate more frequent and more powerful weather events – droughts, floods, storms and heat waves. It is also widely expected that they will lead over time to rises in sea-level, changes to rainfall patterns and river flows. These physical effects will have an impact on the livelihoods of people in most parts of the world, and most of that impact will be negative, though some will gain. The effect will be hardest on the poorest, not only because the lottery of climate will work against them, but because they have less protection due to bad governance and poor infrastructure. In some areas, interacting with other problems in society, the consequences of climate change significantly increase the risk of armed conflict and political instability.

MONGOLIA

NORTH KOREA

JAPAN

SOUTH KOREA

CHINA

NEPAL BHUTAN

Hong Kong SAR TAIWAN

BANGLADESH

BURMA LAOS

THAILAND VIETNAM

CAMBODIA

PHILIPPINES

SRI LANKA

MALAYSIA

INDONESIA

EAST TIMOR

PAPUA NEW GUINEA

AUSTRALIA

NEW ZEALAND

NORTHERN MARIANA IS.

GUAM

MICRONESIA, FED. STATES OF

SOLOMON ISLANDS

TOKELAU

AMERICAN SAMOA

SAMOA

VANUATU

FIJI

COOK ISLANDS

NEW CALEDONIA

TONGA NIUE

Water shortage in certain areas will be one of the most devastating effects of climate change. People may be forced to migrate across borders in search of water and food.

Exposure to climate change

As assessed by the International Panel on Climate Change *2007*

- serious to extreme
- moderate to significant

Extinction

Current trends suggest that between 20% and 33% of all species are at risk of extinction by 2100. Some research suggests 50% are at risk. That would be a mass extinction on the scale of the end of the age of the dinosaurs.

Canadian polar bears

Arctic sea ice is shrinking by about 8% each decade. This affects seals, who breed on ice, and polar bears, who hunt seals. Polar bear populations are starting to show a marked decline.

European heatwave

In the European heatwave of 2003, 35,000–52,000 people died from heat-related causes. By the 2040s, half of Europe's summers will be that hot.

Alaskan permafrost

A temperature increase of 3°–4°C since 1950 is having a visible effect in Alaska. Roads and buildings in some areas are subsiding as the permafrost melts.

North American Mosquito

Mosquitoes are entering their winter dormancy 9 days later than in the 1970s, prolonging the period during which they can spread disease.

Atlantic hurricanes

Since the late 1970s, hurricanes have become 70% more energetic. Since the mid-1990s both hurricanes and major storms have become more frequent.

Tropical Andes

On current trends, all Peru's glaciers below 5,500 metres altitude (most of them) will melt by 2015. Two-thirds of Peru's population depends on glacial melt for water. There will be a surfeit of water followed by severe continuing shortage.

Floods in Bolivia

Heavy rain and flooding early in 2006 affected around 17,500 people.

Drought in southern Brazil

Drought conditions in 2006 led to a 10% decrease in soybean yield.

South Atlantic hurricane

The first hurricane ever observed in the South Atlantic hit Brazil in 2004.

Larsen B ice shelf

In 2002, 1,250 square miles (3,250 sq km) of ice shelf broke away from the Antarctic Peninsula. This was followed by an unexpectedly rapid increase in the rate of glacial flow and ice sheet retreat.

Scientific consensus has been growing that climate change is happening, that it is caused by the global warming created by greenhouse gases – primarily carbon dioxide – produced by human activity, that its effects are being felt already, and that most of its consequences are negative for today's societies. There are some scientists who question each of these conclusions, but observed changes in the climate in different parts of the world are consistent with the theories, models and projections of global warming, and are not adequately explained by any alternative theories and models.

For non-scientists, the safe bet is that climate change is real and reflected in items that make the news headlines – natural disasters, food crises, record summers and more. The question – and the challenge before us – is whether political leaders will deploy the formidable store of human knowledge to mitigate and adapt to climate change, enabling us slowly to work our way towards a global environment we can confidently say is sustainable.

Warning Signs

Siberian melt

Average temperatures in the west have risen by 3°C since the 1960s, leading to melting of the permafrost.

Drought in China

In 2006, severe drought in the north led to 12% of the nation's agriculture being affected. Severe drought in the south affected 18 million people.

Time-lag

Carbon dioxide and the other greenhouse gases stay in the atmosphere for a long time. We are living with the consequences of emissions since the industrial revolution in the early 19th century. In 100 years' time, the world will be living with the consequences of ours.

European butterfly ranges

Of 35 European non-migratory butterfly species studied, 22 shifted their ranges north by 20–150 miles (35–240 km) during the 20th century, and only one shifted south.

Floods in China

Heavy rain led to severe flooding and landslides in June 2006, affecting 17 million people in southern China.

Changing patterns of disease

Flooding in eastern Africa in 2007 created new breeding sites for mosquitoes, causing Rift Valley Fever epidemics and increased malaria.

Asian summer monsoon

Heavy rain and flooding in parts of northern India, Nepal and Bangladesh in 2004 left 1,800 dead and millions stranded. Floods hit again in 2007, leaving over 4,000 dead and 6 million homeless.

Drought in Africa

In 2006 at least 11 million people were affected by food shortages caused by drought in Burundi, Djibouti, Eritrea, Ethiopia, Kenya, Somalia and Tanzania.

South Asian cyclone

In 2008, cyclone Nargis struck the Irrawaddy delta region of Burma, killing at least 100,000 people, and having a devastating effect on the homes and livelihoods of 1.4 million more.

Coral bleaching

Warm seas in 1998 bleached coral in the Australian Great Barrier Reef, destroyed 90% of the coral in the Maldives in the Indian Ocean, and caused scarring visible from space. The scale of the damage was unprecedented. Further and worse damage occurred in 2000 (Fiji), 2002 (Great Barrier Reef) and 2005 (Caribbean).

South Asian heatwave

More than 1,500 fatalities in India and Pakistan in 2003 were caused by temperatures over 50°C.

Madagascan lemurs

Lemurs are among animals producing their young at what is now the "wrong" time. Their breeding season is no longer synchronized with the growing season and the availability of food, putting their survival at risk.

Drought in Australia

A decade of drought has severely affected cattle farmers and reduced rice production by 98%, contributing to international rice shortages, price increases and the gathering food crisis of 2008.

Children in a public primary school in Rwanda where the average class size is 60.

Countries	Official capital	Land area 1,000 hectares 2008	Population		Migrants People born outside country (excl. refugees) as % of population 2005	Life expectanc at birth 2005
			1,000s 2005	Urban as % of total 2006		
Afghanistan	Kabul	65,209	29,929	23%	0.1%	47.0
Albania	Tirane	2,740	3,563	46%	2.6%	75.5
Algeria	Algiers	238,174	32,532	64%	0.7%	71.7
Angola	Luanda	124,670	11,191	54%	0.4%	41.4
Antigua and Barbuda	Saint John's	44	69	40%	22.4%	75.3
Argentina	Buenos Aires	273,669	39,538	90%	3.9%	74.8
Armenia	Yerevan	2,820	2,983	64%	7.8%	73.3
Australia	Canberra	768,230	20,090	88%	20.3%	80.6
Austria	Vienna	8,245	8,185	66%	15.1%	79.4
Azerbaijan	Baku	8,266	7,912	52%	2.2%	72.3
Bahamas	Nassau	1,001	302	91%	9.8%	71.0
Bahrain	Al-Manámah	71	688	97%	40.7%	74.9
Bangladesh	Dhaka	13,017	144,320	26%	0.7%	63.9
Barbados	Bridgetown	43	279	53%	9.7%	74.9
Belarus	Mensk	20,748	10,300	73%	12.2%	68.5
Belgium	Brussels	3,023	10,364	97%	6.9%	79.5
Belize	Belmopan	2,281	279	49%	15.0%	71.8
Benin	Porto-Novo	11,062	7,460	41%	2.1%	55.0
Bhutan	Thimphu	4,700	2,232	11%	0.5%	63.5
Bolivia	La Paz	108,438	8,858	65%	1.3%	64.8
Bosnia and Herzegovina	Sarajevo	5,120	4,025	46%	1.0%	74.4
Botswana	Gaborone	56,673	1,545	58%	4.5%	35.0
Brazil	Brasilia	845,942	186,113	85%	0.3%	71.2
Brunei	Bandar Seri Begawan	527	372	74%	33.2%	77.0
Bulgaria	Sofia	10,864	7,450	70%	1.3%	72.6
Burkina Faso	Ouagadougou	27,360	13,925	19%	5.8%	48.5
Burma	Nay Pyi Taw	65,755	42,909	31%	0.2%	61.1
Burundi	Bujumbura	2,568	6,371	10%	1.3%	44.6
Cambodia	Phnom Penh	17,652	13,607	20%	2.2%	57.0
Cameroon	Yaoundé	46,540	16,380	55%	0.8%	46.1
Canada	Ottawa	909,351	32,805	80%	18.9%	80.2
Cape Verde	Praia	403	418	58%	2.2%	70.7
Central African Republic	Bangui	62,300	3,800	38%	1.9%	39.4
Chad	N'Djamena	125,920	9,826	26%	4.5%	44.0
Chile	Santiago	74,880	15,981	88%	1.4%	78.2
China	Beijing	932,749	1,306,314	41%	0.0%	71.8
Colombia	Santafé de Bogotá	110,950	42,954	73%	0.3%	72.8
Comoros	Moroni	186	671	38%	8.4%	62.6
Congo	Brazzaville	34,150	3,039	61%	7.2%	52.8
Congo, Dem. Rep.	Kinshasa	226,705	60,085	33%	0.9%	44.0
Cook Islands	Avarua	24	21	–	17.0%	–
Costa Rica	San José	5,106	4,016	62%	10.2%	78.9
Côte d'Ivoire	Yamoussoukro	31,800	17,693	45%	13.1%	46.2
Croatia	Zagreb	5,592	4,496	57%	14.5%	75.7
Cuba	Havana	10,982	11,347	75%	0.7%	77.3
Cyprus	Lefkosia (Nicosia)	924	780	70%	13.9%	79.3
Czech Republic	Prague	7,726	10,241	74%	4.4%	75.9

Indicators of Wellbeing

Gross National Income GNI per capita 2005–06 current international $	Water % with access to improved source 2004	Literacy % of adult population who are literate 2005	Education Net enrolment in primary school 2005 or latest available	Maternal mortality Deaths in childbirth per 100,000 live births 2006	Undernourished people As % of population 2002–04	Countries
–	–	–	–	–	–	Afghanistan
5,840	96%	99%	–	17	6%	Albania
6,900	85%	70%	97%	38	4%	Algeria
2,360	53%	67%	–	260	35%	Angola
13,500	91%	86%	–	11	–	Antigua and Barbuda
15,390	96%	97%	99%	16	3%	Argentina
5,890	92%	99%	79%	24	24%	Armenia
34,060	100%	–	97%	6	<2.5%	Australia
35,130	100%	–	97%	5	<2.5%	Austria
5,960	77%	99%	85%	88	7%	Azerbaijan
–	97%	–	91%	14	8%	Bahamas
18,770	–	87%	97%	10	–	Bahrain
2,340	74%	48%	94%	69	30%	Bangladesh
–	100%	–	98%	12	<2.5%	Barbados
8,810	100%	100%	89%	13	4%	Belarus
35,090	–	–	99%	4	<2.5%	Belgium
6,650	91%	75%	94%	16	4%	Belize
1,160	67%	35%	78%	148	12%	Benin
5,690	62%	47%	–	70	–	Bhutan
2,890	85%	87%	94%	61	23%	Bolivia
–	97%	97%	–	15	9%	Bosnia and Herzegovina
12,250	95%	81%	85%	124	32%	Botswana
8,800	90%	89%	95%	20	7%	Brazil
–	–	93%	93%	9	4%	Brunei
10,140	99%	98%	93%	14	8%	Bulgaria
1,330	61%	24%	45%	204	15%	Burkina Faso
–	78%	90%	90%	104	5%	Burma
710	79%	59%	60%	181	66%	Burundi
2,920	41%	74%	99%	82	33%	Cambodia
2,370	66%	68%	–	149	26%	Cameroon
34,610	100%	–	99%	6	<2.5	Canada
5,980	80%	81%	90%	34	–	Cape Verde
1,280	75%	49%	–	175	44%	Central African Republic
1,230	42%	26%	61%	209	35%	Chad
11,270	95%	96%	90%	9	4%	Chile
7,740	77%	91%	–	24	12%	China
7,620	93%	93%	87%	21	13%	Colombia
2,010	86%	–	55%	68	60%	Comoros
870	58%	85%	44%	126	33%	Congo
720	46%	67%	–	205	74%	Congo, Dem. Rep.
–	–	–	–	–	–	Cook Islands
10,770	97%	95%	–	12	5%	Costa Rica
1,550	84%	49%	56%	127	13%	Côte d'Ivoire
13,680	100%	98%	87%	6	7%	Croatia
–	91%	100%	97%	7	<2.5%	Cuba
21,490	100%	97%	99%	4	<2.5%	Cyprus
21,470	100%	–	92%	4	<2.5%	Czech Republic

Countries	Official capital	Land area 1,000 hectares *2008*	Population		Migrants People born outside country (excl. refugees) as % of population *2005*	Life expectancy at birth *2005*
			1,000s *2005*	Urban as % of total *2006*		
Denmark	Copenhagen	4,243	5,432	86%	7.2%	77.8
Djibouti	Djibouti	2,318	477	87%	2.6%	53.4
Dominica	Roseau	75	69	73%	5.7%	76.6
Dominican Republic	Santo Domingo	4,838	8,950	68%	1.8%	70.9
East Timor	Dili	1,487	1,041	27%	0.6%	56.7
Ecuador	Quito	27,684	13,364	63%	0.9%	74.7
Egypt	Cairo	99,545	77,506	43%	0.2%	70.5
El Salvador	San Salvador	2,072	6,705	60%	0.3%	71.3
Equatorial Guinea	Malabo	2,805	536	39%	1.2%	42.3
Eritrea	Asmara	10,100	4,562	20%	0.3%	54.9
Estonia	Tallinn	4,239	1,333	69%	15.2%	72.6
Ethiopia	Addis Ababa	100,000	69,114	16%	0.7%	42.7
Fiji	Suva	1,827	893	51%	2.0%	68.3
Finland	Helsinki	30,459	5,223	61%	3.0%	78.8
France	Paris	55,010	60,656	77%	10.7%	80.2
Gabon	Libreville	25,767	1,389	84%	17.7%	53.8
Gambia	Banjul	1,000	1,593	55%	15.3%	56.8
Georgia	Tbilisi	6,949	4,677	52%	4.3%	71.3
Germany	Berlin	34,877	82,431	75%	12.3%	78.9
Ghana	Accra	22,754	21,030	49%	7.5%	57.5
Greece	Athens	12,890	10,668	59%	8.8%	79.0
Grenada	St George's	34	90	31%	10.5%	73.0
Guatemala	Guatemala City	10,843	14,655	48%	0.4%	67.9
Guinea	Conakry	24,572	9,468	33%	4.3%	54.1
Guinea-Bissau	Bissau	2,812	1,416	30%	1.2%	45.1
Guyana	Georgetown	19,685	711	28%	0.1%	64.3
Haiti	Port-au-Prince	2,756	7,790	39%	0.4%	52.6
Honduras	Tegucigalpa	11,189	6,975	47%	0.4%	68.6
Hungary	Budapest	8,961	10,007	67%	3.1%	72.6
Iceland	Reykjavik	10,025	297	93%	7.8%	81.1
India	New Delhi	297,319	1,080,264	29%	0.5%	63.5
Indonesia	Jakarta	181,157	241,974	49%	0.1%	67.8
Iran	Tehran	162,855	68,018	67%	2.8%	71.1
Iraq	Baghdad	43,737	26,075	67%	0.1%	60.0
Ireland	Dublin	6,889	4,016	61%	14.1%	79.4
Israel	Jerusalem	2,164	6,277	92%	39.6%	79.7
Italy	Rome	29,411	58,103	68%	4.3%	80.3
Jamaica	Kingston	1,083	2,732	53%	0.7%	70.9
Japan	Tokyo	36,450	127,417	66%	1.6%	82.1
Jordan	Amman	8,824	5,760	83%	39.0%	72.0
Kazakhstan	Astana	269,970	15,186	58%	16.9%	66.2
Kenya	Nairobi	56,914	32,368	21%	1.0%	49.0
Kiribati	Tarawa	81	103	48%	2.6%	62.8
Korea, North	Pyongyang	12,041	22,912	62%	0.2%	63.9
Korea, South	Seoul	9,873	48,893	81%	1.2%	77.6
Kuwait	Kuwait City	1,782	2,336	98%	62.1%	77.5
Kyrgyzstan	Bishkek	19,180	5,146	36%	5.5%	68.3

Indicators of Wellbeing

Gross National Income GNI per capita 2005–06 current international $	Water % with access to improved source 2004	Literacy % of adult population who are literate 2005	Education Net enrolment in primary school 2005 or latest available	Maternal mortality Deaths in childbirth per 100,000 live births 2006	Undernourished people As % of population 2002–04	Countries
36,460	100%	–	95%	5	<2.5%	Denmark
2,540	73%	–	33%	130	24%	Djibouti
6,490	97%	88%	84%	15	8%	Dominica
8,290	95%	87%	88%	29	29%	Dominican Republic
–	58%	50%	98%	55	9%	East Timor
4,400	94%	91%	98%	24	6%	Ecuador
4,690	98%	71%	94%	35	4%	Egypt
5,340	84%	81%	93%	25	11%	El Salvador
10,150	43%	87%	81%	206	–	Equatorial Guinea
1,090	60%	–	47%	74	75%	Eritrea
17,540	100%	100%	95%	7	<2.5%	Estonia
1,190	22%	36%	61%	123	46%	Ethiopia
6,200	47%	–	96%	18	5%	Fiji
35,150	100%	–	98%	4	<2.5%	Finland
33,740	100%	–	99%	4	<2.5%	France
5,310	88%	84%	77%	91	5%	Gabon
1,970	82%	–	77%	113	29%	Gambia
3,690	82%	100%	93%	32	9%	Georgia
31,830	100%	–	96%	4	<2.5%	Germany
2,640	75%	58%	65%	120	11%	Ghana
24,560	–	96%	99%	4	<2.5%	Greece
7,810	95%	96%	84%	20	7%	Grenada
4,800	95%	69%	94%	41	22%	Guatemala
2,410	50%	30%	66%	161	24%	Guinea
830	59%	–	45%	200	39%	Guinea-Bissau
4,680	83%	–	–	62	8%	Guyana
1,490	54%	–	–	80	46%	Haiti
3,540	87%	80%	91%	27	23%	Honduras
18,290	99%	–	89%	7	<2.5%	Hungary
36,560	100%	–	99%	3	<2.5%	Iceland
3,800	86%	61%	–	76	20%	India
3,950	77%	90%	96%	34	6%	Indonesia
8,490	94%	82%	95%	34	4%	Iran
–	–	–	88%	–	–	Iraq
35,900	–	–	96%	5	<2.5%	Ireland
23,700	100%	97%	97%	5	<2.5%	Israel
30,550	–	98%	99%	4	<2.5%	Italy
4,030	93%	80%	90%	31	9%	Jamaica
33,150	100%	–	100%	4	<2.5%	Japan
6,210	97%	91%	89%	25	6%	Jordan
7,780	86%	100%	91%	29	6%	Kazakhstan
1,300	61%	74%	79%	121	31%	Kenya
8,970	–	–	97%	64	–	Kiribati
–	–	–	–	55	–	Korea, North
23,800	92%	–	99%	5	<2.5%	Korea, South
26,790	–	93%	87%	11	5%	Kuwait
1,990	77%	99%	87%	41	4%	Kyrgyzstan

Countries	Official capital	Land area 1,000 hectares 2008	Population		Migrants People born outside country (excl. refugees) as % of population 2005	Life expectancy at birth 2005
			1,000s 2005	Urban as % of total 2006		
Laos	Vientiane	23,080	6,217	21%	0.4%	61.9
Latvia	Riga	6,229	2,290	68%	19.5%	71.4
Lebanon	Beirut	1,023	3,826	87%	18.4%	72.5
Lesotho	Maseru	3,035	1,867	19%	0.3%	35.2
Liberia	Monrovia	9,632	3,482	59%	1.5%	42.5
Libya	Tripoli	175,954	5,766	85%	10.5%	74.4
Lithuania	Vilnius	6,268	3,597	67%	4.8%	71.3
Luxembourg	Luxembourg	259	469	83%	37.4%	79.2
Macedonia	Skopje	2,543	2,079	70%	6.0%	73.8
Madagascar	Antananarivo	58,154	18,040	27%	0.3%	55.8
Malawi	Lilongwe	9,408	12,159	18%	2.2%	40.5
Malaysia	Kuala Lumpur	32,855	23,953	68%	6.5%	73.7
Maldives	Malé	30	349	30%	1.0%	67.6
Mali	Bamako	122,019	12,292	31%	0.3%	48.6
Malta	Valletta	32	399	96%	2.7%	79.5
Marshall Islands	Majuro	18	59	67%	2.7%	–
Mauritania	Nouakchott	103,070	3,087	41%	2.1%	53.7
Mauritius	Port Louis	203	1,231	42%	1.7%	73.0
Mexico	Mexico City	194,395	106,203	76%	0.6%	75.4
Micronesia, Fed. Sts.	Palikir	70	108	22%	3.2%	68.1
Moldova	Chisinau	3,287	4,455	47%	10.5%	68.3
Mongolia	Ulaan Baatar	156,650	2,791	57%	0.3%	66.8
Montenegro*	Podgorica	1,381	678	52%	4.9%	74.1
Morocco	Rabat	44,630	32,726	59%	0.4%	70.4
Mozambique	Maputo	78,638	19,027	35%	2.1%	41.8
Namibia	Windhoek	82,329	1,976	36%	7.1%	46.9
Nepal	Kathmandu	14,300	27,677	16%	3.0%	62.7
Netherlands	Amsterdam	3,388	16,407	81%	10.1%	79.3
New Zealand	Wellington	26,771	4,035	86%	15.9%	79.6
Nicaragua	Managua	12,140	5,465	59%	0.5%	70.4
Niger	Niamey	126,670	11,666	17%	0.9%	44.9
Nigeria	Abuja	91,077	140,602	49%	0.7%	46.6
Norway	Oslo	30,428	4,593	78%	7.4%	80.0
Oman	Muscat	30,950	3,002	72%	24.4%	74.8
Pakistan	Islamabad	77,088	162,420	35%	2.1%	64.9
Palestine Authority	–	602	2,386	72%	45.4%	73.4
Panama	Panama City	7,443	3,039	72%	3.2%	75.2
Papua New Guinea	Port Moresby	45,286	5,545	14%	0.4%	56.4
Paraguay	Asunción	39,730	6,348	59%	2.7%	71.4
Peru	Lima	128,000	27,926	73%	0.1%	70.7
Philippines	Manila	29,817	87,857	63%	0.5%	71.0
Poland	Warsaw	30,633	38,635	62%	1.8%	75.0
Portugal	Lisbon	9,150	10,566	58%	7.3%	78.1
Puerto Rico	San Juan	887	3,917	98%	10.6%	77.6
Qatar	Doha	1,100	863	95%	78.3%	74.1
Romania	Bucharest	22,998	22,330	54%	0.6%	71.7
Russia	Moscow	1,638,139	143,155	73%	8.4%	65.5

* Data for Serbia and Montenegro on urban population, migrant population and school enrolment pre-date their separation in 2006 and apply to the country as a single entity.

Indicators of Wellbeing

Gross National Income GNI per capita 2005–06 current international $	Water % with access to improved source 2004	Literacy % of adult population who are literate 2005	Education Net enrolment in primary school 2005 or latest available	Maternal mortality Deaths in childbirth per 100,000 live births 2006	Undernourished people As % of population 2002–04	Countries
2,050	51%	69%	84%	75	19%	Laos
15,350	99%	100%	88%	9	3%	Latvia
5,460	100%	–	92%	30	3%	Lebanon
4,340	79%	82%	87%	132	13%	Lesotho
–	–	–	66%	235	–	Liberia
–	–	84%	–	18	<2.5%	Libya
14,930	–	100%	89%	8	<2.5%	Lithuania
–	100%	–	95%	4	<2.5%	Luxembourg
7,610	–	96%	92%	17	5%	Macedonia
960	50%	71%	92%	115	38%	Madagascar
720	73%	64%	95%	120	35%	Malawi
11,300	99%	89%	95%	12	3%	Malaysia
–	83%	96%	79%	30	10%	Maldives
1,130	50%	24%	51%	217	29%	Mali
18,020	100%	88%	86%	6	<2.5%	Malta
–	–	–	90%	56	–	Marshall Islands
2,600	53%	51%	72%	125	10%	Mauritania
13,510	100%	84%	95%	14	5%	Mauritius
11,410	97%	92%	98%	35	5%	Mexico
7,830	–	–	–	41	–	Micronesia, Fed. Sts.
2,880	92%	99%	86%	19	11%	Moldova
2,280	62%	98%	84%	43	27%	Mongolia
–	–	–	96%	10	–	Montenegro*
5,000	81%	52%	86%	37	6%	Morocco
1,220	43%	39%	77%	138	44%	Mozambique
8,110	87%	85%	72%	61	24%	Namibia
1,630	90%	49%	79%	59	17%	Nepal
37,580	100%	–	99%	5	<2.5%	Netherlands
27,220	–	–	99%	6	<2.5%	New Zealand
4,010	79%	77%	87%	36	27%	Nicaragua
830	46%	29%	40%	253	32%	Niger
1,050	48%	69%	68%	191	9%	Nigeria
43,820	100%	–	98%	4	<2.5%	Norway
14,570	–	81%	76%	12	–	Oman
2,500	91%	50%	68%	97	24%	Pakistan
–	92%	92%	80%	22	16%	Palestine Authority
7,680	90%	92%	98%	23	23%	Panama
2,410	39%	57%	–	73	–	Papua New Guinea
5,070	86%	94%	88%	22	15%	Paraguay
6,080	83%	88%	96%	25	12%	Peru
5,980	85%	93%	94%	32	18%	Philippines
14,830	–	–	96%	7	<2.5%	Poland
21,580	–	94%	98%	5	<2.5%	Portugal
–	–	–	–	–	–	Puerto Rico
–	100%	89%	96%	21	–	Qatar
9,820	57%	97%	93%	18	<2.5%	Romania
11,630	97%	99%	92%	16	3%	Russia

Countries	Official capital	Land area 1,000 hectares 2008	Population 1,000s 2005	Population Urban as % of total 2006	Migrants People born outside country (excl. refugees) as % of population 2005	Life expectanc at birth 2005
Rwanda	Kigali	2,467	8,099	20%	1.3%	44.1
Samoa	Apia	283	177	23%	5.0%	70.7
São Tomé and Principe	São Tomé	96	187	59%	4.8%	63.5
Saudi Arabia	Riyadh	214,969	26,418	81%	25.9%	72.6
Senegal	Dakar	19,253	11,127	42%	2.8%	56.5
Serbia*	Belgrade	7,747	10,159	52%	4.9%	72.8
Seychelles	Victoria	46	81	53%	6.1%	73.0
Sierra Leone	Freetown	7,162	6,018	41%	2.2%	41.4
Singapore	Singapore	69	4,426	100%	42.6%	79.7
Slovakia	Bratislava	4,810	5,431	56%	2.3%	73.9
Slovenia	Ljubljana	2,014	2,011	51%	8.5%	77.6
Solomon Islands	Honiara	2,799	538	17%	0.7%	62.9
Somalia	Mogadishu	62,734	8,592	36%	3.4%	47.7
South Africa	Pretoria	121,447	42,552	60%	2.3%	47.7
Spain	Madrid	49,919	40,341	77%	11.1%	80.6
Sri Lanka	Colombo	6,463	20,065	15%	1.8%	74.7
St. Kitts and Nevis	Basseterre	–	39	32%	10.4%	71.3
St. Lucia	Castries	–	166	28%	5.4%	74.2
St. Vincent and Grenadines	Kingstown	–	118	46%	8.7%	72.3
Sudan	Khartoum	237,600	40,187	42%	1.8%	56.7
Suriname	Paramaribo	15,600	438	74%	1.2%	69.7
Swaziland	Mbabane	1,720	1,174	24%	4.4%	41.5
Sweden	Stockholm	41,033	9,002	84%	12.4%	80.5
Switzerland	Bern	4,000	7,489	76%	22.9%	81.2
Syria	Damascus	18,378	18,449	51%	5.2%	73.8
Tajikistan	Dushanbe	13,996	7,164	25%	4.7%	64.0
Tanzania	Dar es Salaam	88,580	37,323	25%	2.1%	46.3
Thailand	Bangkok	51,089	65,444	33%	1.6%	70.9
Togo	Lomé	5,439	5,682	41%	3.0%	55.1
Tonga	Nuku'alofa	72	112	24%	1.1%	72.6
Trinidad and Tobago	Port-of-Spain	513	1,089	13%	2.9%	70.0
Tunisia	Tunis	15,536	10,075	66%	0.4%	73.5
Turkey	Ankara	76,963	69,661	68%	1.8%	71.3
Turkmenistan	Ashgabat	46,993	4,952	47%	4.6%	62.9
Uganda	Kampala	19,710	27,202	13%	1.8%	50.0
Ukraine	Kyiv	57,938	47,425	68%	14.7%	68.0
United Arab Emirates	Abu Dhabi	8,360	2,563	77%	71.4%	79.2
United Kingdom	London	24,193	60,441	90%	9.1%	78.9
United States	Washington D.C.	916,192	295,734	81%	12.9%	77.7
Uruguay	Montevideo	17,502	3,416	92%	2.4%	75.6
Uzbekistan	Tashkent	42,540	26,851	37%	4.8%	67.4
Vanuatu	Port-Vila	1,219	206	24%	0.5%	69.5
Venezuela	Caracas	88,205	25,375	94%	3.8%	74.2
Vietnam	Hanoi	31,007	83,770	27%	0.0%	70.7
Yemen	Sanaá	52,797	20,727	28%	1.3%	61.7
Zambia	Lusaka	74,339	10,614	35%	2.4%	38.4
Zimbabwe	Harare	38,685	12,747	36%	3.9%	37.3

* Data for Serbia and Montenegro on urban population, migrant population and school enrolment pre-date their separation in 2006 and apply to the country as a single entity.

Indicators of Wellbeing

Gross National Income GNI per capita 2005–06 current international $	Water % with access to improved source 2004	Literacy % of adult population who are literate 2005	Education Net enrolment in primary school 2005 or latest available	Maternal mortality Deaths in childbirth per 100,000 live births 2006	Undernourished people As % of population 2002–04	Countries
1,270	74%	65%	74%	160	33%	Rwanda
6,400	88%	99%	90%	28	4%	Samoa
–	79%	85%	–	96	10%	São Tomé and Principe
15,550	–	83%	78%	25	4%	Saudi Arabia
1,840	76%	39%	69%	116	20%	Senegal
–	–	–	96%	8	–	Serbia*
16,560	88%	92%	99%	13	9%	Seychelles
850	57%	35%	–	270	51%	Sierra Leone
31,710	100%	93%	–	3	–	Singapore
17,600	100%	–	92%	8	7%	Slovakia
23,970	–	100%	98%	4	3%	Slovenia
2,170	70%	77%	63%	73	21%	Solomon Islands
–	–	–	–	145	–	Somalia
11,710	88%	82%	87%	69	<2.5%	South Africa
28,030	100%	97%	99%	4	<2.5%	Spain
5,010	79%	91%	97%	13	22%	Sri Lanka
12,690	100%	98%	93%	19	10%	St. Kitts and Nevis
6,970	98%	95%	–	14	5%	St. Lucia
7,010	–	88%	90%	20	10%	St. Vincent and Grenadines
2,160	70%	61%	43%	89	26%	Sudan
8,120	92%	90%	94%	39	8%	Suriname
5,170	62%	80%	80%	164	22%	Swaziland
35,070	100%	–	96%	3	<2.5%	Sweden
40,930	100%	–	93%	5	<2.5%	Switzerland
3,930	93%	81%	95%	14	4%	Syria
1,410	59%	100%	97%	68	56%	Tajikistan
740	62%	69%	91%	118	44%	Tanzania
9,140	99%	93%	–	8	22%	Thailand
1,490	52%	53%	78%	108	24%	Togo
8,580	100%	99%	95%	24	–	Tonga
16,260	91%	98%	90%	38	10%	Trinidad and Tobago
8,490	93%	74%	97%	23	<2.5%	Tunisia
9,060	96%	87%	89%	26	3%	Turkey
–	72%	99%	–	51	7%	Turkmenistan
1,490	60%	67%	–	134	19%	Uganda
7,520	96%	99%	83%	24	<2.5%	Ukraine
23,990	100%	89%	71%	8	<2.5%	United Arab Emirates
35,580	100%	–	99%	6	<2.5%	United Kingdom
44,260	100%	–	92%	8	<2.5%	United States
11,150	100%	97%	93%	12	<2.5%	Uruguay
2,250	82%	–	–	43	25%	Uzbekistan
3,280	60%	74%	94%	36	11%	Vanuatu
7,440	83%	93%	91%	21	18%	Venezuela
3,300	85%	90%	88%	17	16%	Vietnam
920	67%	54%	75%	100	38%	Yemen
1,000	58%	68%	89%	182	46%	Zambia
2,030	81%	89%	82%	105	47%	Zimbabwe

Countries	GDP Total US$ millions 2006 or latest available	Trade As % of GDP 2006		Investment Net inflow of FDI as % of GDP 2005	Aid Amount received as % of GDP 2005	Military expenditure 2006	
		goods	services			total	as % of GDP
Afghanistan	8,399	39%	–	–	37.9%	143	1.7%
Albania	9,098	42%	34%	3.1%	3.7%	141	1.5%
Algeria	114,727	64%	–	1.1%	0.4%	3,096	2.7%
Angola	45,163	106%	21%	–4.0%	1.5%	1,588	4.7%
Antigua and Barbuda	998	63%	76%	–	0.9%	5	5.5%
Argentina	214,241	38%	7%	2.6%	0.1%	1,873	0.9%
Armenia	6,387	50%	12%	5.3%	3.9%	184	2.9%
Australia	780,531	34%	8%	–4.7%	–	17,208	2.4%
Austria	322,001	86%	24%	3.0%	–	2,630	0.8%
Azerbaijan	19,851	54%	25%	12.7%	1.9%	658	3.3%
Bahamas	5,502	–	60%	–	–	40	0.7%
Bahrain	16,041	–	20%	–	1.0%	532	3.4%
Bangladesh	61,897	45%	6%	1.3%	2.1%	938	1.6%
Barbados	3,430	–	69%	2.0%	–0.1%	25	0.7%
Belarus	36,945	114%	10%	1.0%	0.2%	279	0.8%
Belgium	394,033	186%	29%	8.6%	–	4,428	1.1%
Belize	1,214	77%	41%	11.4%	1.3%	18	1.5%
Benin	4,775	33%	12%	0.5%	8.2%	47	1.0%
Bhutan	942	72%	–	0.1%	11.1%	–	–
Bolivia	11,162	60%	12%	–2.9%	6.4%	156	1.4%
Bosnia and Herzegovina	12,255	94%	14%	3.0%	5.3%	142	1.2%
Botswana	10,598	75%	16%	2.7%	0.7%	289	3.0%
Brazil	1,067,472	21%	5%	1.7%	0.0%	16,206	1.5%
Brunei	11,562	–	–	–	–	328	2.8%
Bulgaria	31,483	121%	29%	9.6%	2.5%	703	2.3%
Burkina Faso	6,173	30%	7%	0.3%	11.6%	85	1.4%
Burma	–	–	–	–	–	6,920	18.7%
Burundi	903	59%	18%	0.1%	47.0%	49	5.1%
Cambodia	7,258	121%	28%	6.1%	9.0%	123	1.7%
Cameroon	18,323	38%	15%	0.1%	2.5%	257	1.4%
Canada	1,271,593	60%	10%	3.1%	–	14,958	1.2%
Cape Verde	1,144	49%	49%	5.4%	16.6%	7	0.6%
Central African Republic	1,494	22%	–	0.4%	7.0%	16	1.0%
Chad	6,541	76%	–	12.0%	7.8%	59	0.9%
Chile	145,843	67%	11%	5.6%	0.1%	4,677	3.2%
China	2,644,681	66%	7%	3.5%	0.1%	121,872	1.3%
Colombia	153,405	37%	7%	8.4%	0.4%	5,377	4.0%
Comoros	403	30%	–	0.3%	6.6%	–	–
Congo	7,385	116%	30%	12.1%	32.5%	84	1.2%
Congo, Dem. Rep.	8,543	60%	–	5.7%	27.0%	163	1.0%
Cook Islands	–	–	–	–	–	–	–
Costa Rica	22,229	89%	21%	4.3%	0.2%	99	0.4%
Côte d'Ivoire	17,551	80%	18%	1.7%	0.8%	266	1.5%
Croatia	42,925	75%	34%	4.5%	0.3%	693	1.6%
Cuba	–	–	–	–	–	1,660	4.0%
Cyprus	18,371	–	58%	–	0.4%	240	1.3%
Czech Republic	143,018	133%	16%	–	0.3%	2,464	1.7%

Economy and Environment

Energy Use Oil equivalent 2004		CO$_2$ Emissions Tonnes of CO$_2$ 2004		Water		Countries
total tonnes	kg per capita	total	per capita	Cubic metres of annual renewable water available per capita 2007	Cubic metres withdrawn per capita 2007	
–	–	0.7	0.0	2,015	1,014	Afghanistan
2	760	5.2	1.7	13,184	544	Albania
33	1,017	91.6	2.8	423	194	Algeria
9	613	19.8	1.3	10,909	26	Angola
–	–	0.4	5.1	619	78	Antigua and Barbuda
64	1,660	145.6	3.8	20,591	765	Argentina
2	704	3.7	1.2	3,511	960	Armenia
116	5,762	350.9	17.5	23,911	1,224	Australia
33	4,060	76.8	9.4	9,455	260	Austria
13	1,559	30.9	3.7	3,547	2,079	Azerbaijan
–	–	2.0	6.3	60	–	Bahamas
7	10,469	16.4	22.9	155	423	Bahrain
23	164	37.5	0.3	8,232	552	Bangladesh
–	–	1.4	5.3	295	297	Barbados
27	2,725	65.9	6.7	6,014	281	Belarus
58	5,536	119.2	11.4	1,751	916	Belgium
–	–	0.8	2.8	66,268	478	Belize
2	303	2.4	0.3	2,765	20	Benin
–	–	0.5	0.8	42,035	192	Bhutan
5	553	12.2	1.4	65,358	161	Bolivia
5	1,203	15.7	4.0	9,566	–	Bosnia and Herzegovina
2	1,055	4.4	2.5	8,215	110	Botswana
205	1,114	346.2	1.9	43,028	336	Brazil
3	7,370	8.9	24.4	21,795	296	Brunei
19	2,434	47.4	6.1	2,797	1,318	Bulgaria
–	–	1.1	0.1	890	62	Burkina Faso
14	283	10.2	0.2	20,313	680	Burma
–	–	0.2	0.0	442	44	Burundi
–	–	0.5	0.0	32,526	296	Cambodia
7	433	6.9	0.4	16,920	63	Cameroon
269	8,411	549.1	17.0	88,336	1,470	Canada
–	–	0.3	0.6	566	48	Cape Verde
–	–	0.3	0.1	34,787	5	Central African Republic
–	–	0.1	0.0	4,174	28	Chad
28	1,732	63.4	3.9	55,425	803	Chile
1,609	1,242	5,204.8	4.0	2,125	484	China
28	625	61.7	1.4	45,408	246	Colombia
–	–	0.1	0.1	1,427	13	Comoros
1	274	3.3	0.8	196,319	13	Congo
17	296	2.2	0.0	20,973	7	Congo, Dem. Rep.
–	–	0.0	1.4	–	–	Cook Islands
4	870	6.1	1.4	25,157	655	Costa Rica
7	388	6.4	0.4	4,315	57	Côte d'Ivoire
9	1,985	22.4	5.0	23,161	–	Croatia
11	950	25.8	2.3	3,368	728	Cuba
3	3,535	7.3	9.8	913	302	Cyprus
46	4,460	125.2	12.3	1,290	251	Czech Republic

Countries	GDP Total US$ millions 2006 or latest available	Trade As % of GDP 2006		Investment Net inflow of FDI as % of GDP 2005	Aid Amount received as % of GDP 2005	Military expenditure 2006	
		goods	services			total	as % of GDP
Denmark	275,366	65%	35%	2.0%	–	3,876	1.4%
Djibouti	769	44%	–	3.2%	10.1%	17	2.3%
Dominica	319	68%	47%	9.2%	5.8%	–	–
Dominican Republic	31,846	58%	18%	3.5%	0.3%	256	0.7%
East Timor	356	–	–	–	26.7%	–	–
Ecuador	41,402	58%	9%	4.5%	0.6%	653	1.9%
Egypt	107,484	32%	28%	6.0%	1.0%	4,337	4.0%
El Salvador	18,654	61%	14%	3.0%	1.2%	106	0.6%
Equatorial Guinea	8,565	133%	–	24.7%	1.1%	8	0.1%
Eritrea	1,085	38%	14%	1.2%	36.9%	–	–
Estonia	16,410	135%	36%	21.8%	1.2%	238	1.4%
Ethiopia	13,315	43%	18%	2.3%	17.1%	345	2.6%
Fiji	3,138	89%	–	–0.1%	2.4%	43	1.5%
Finland	210,652	69%	17%	2.1%	–	2,750	1.3%
France	2,248,091	46%	10%	3.3%	–	54,003	2.4%
Gabon	9,546	74%	15%	3.5%	0.8%	21	0.2%
Gambia	511	50%	27%	11.3%	13.0%	2	0.3%
Georgia	7,744	62%	21%	7.0%	4.9%	339	4.4%
Germany	2,896,876	70%	14%	1.1%	–	37,775	1.3%
Ghana	12,906	74%	22%	1.0%	10.6%	83	0.7%
Greece	308,449	34%	21%	0.3%	–	7,286	2.4%
Grenada	525	58%	49%	5.6%	10.4%	–	–
Guatemala	35,325	51%	9%	0.7%	0.8%	146	0.4%
Guinea	3,317	54%	9%	3.1%	5.5%	36	1.2%
Guinea-Bissau	304	61%	19%	3.3%	27.4%	13	4.0%
Guyana	896	161%	43%	9.7%	18.3%	–	–
Haiti	4,975	47%	13%	0.2%	11.7%	–	–
Honduras	9,235	80%	20%	5.6%	8.6%	55	0.6%
Hungary	112,920	133%	23%	5.8%	0.3%	1,323	1.2%
Iceland	16,265	60%	28%	15.6%	–	46	0.3%
India	911,813	33%	8%	0.8%	0.2%	22,428	2.5%
Indonesia	364,790	50%	13%	1.8%	0.9%	3,645	1.0%
Iran	217,898	57%	4%	0.0%	0.1%	7,160	3.3%
Iraq	–	–	–	–	–	–	–
Ireland	220,137	83%	63%	–14.7%	–	1,113	0.5%
Israel	140,457	–	25%	4.5%	0.4%	11,031	7.9%
Italy	1,850,961	46%	10%	1.1%	–	30,635	1.7%
Jamaica	10,023	69%	42%	7.0%	0.4%	57	0.6%
Japan	4,368,435	28%	6%	0.1%	–	41,144	0.9%
Jordan	14,101	117%	38%	12.1%	4.8%	1,115	7.9%
Kazakhstan	81,003	79%	15%	3.5%	0.4%	648	0.8%
Kenya	22,779	51%	16%	0.1%	4.0%	355	1.6%
Kiribati	71	86%	–	–	24.5%	–	–
Korea, North	–	–	–	–	–	–	–
Korea, South	888,024	72%	14%	0.5%	0.0%	24,645	2.8%
Kuwait	80,781	–	17%	0.3%	0.0%	3,497	3.4%
Kyrgyzstan	2,818	92%	22%	1.7%	11.3%	36	1.3%

Economy and Environment

Energy Use Oil equivalent 2004		CO₂ Emissions Tonnes of CO₂ 2004		Water		Countries
total tonnes	kg per capita	total	per capita	Cubic metres of annual renewable water available per capita 2007	Cubic metres withdrawn per capita 2007	
20	3,716	52.6	9.7	1,099	237	Denmark
–	–	0.4	0.5	366	27	Djibouti
–	–	0.1	1.5	–	210	Dominica
8	821	19.5	2.2	2,295	393	Dominican Republic
–	–	–	–	–	–	East Timor
10	773	28.2	2.2	31,739	1,326	Ecuador
57	783	152.2	2.1	759	969	Egypt
4	664	6.4	0.9	3,546	198	El Salvador
–	–	8.9	18.0	49,336	229	Equatorial Guinea
–	–	0.8	0.2	1,338	131	Eritrea
5	3,835	17.9	13.3	9,696	120	Estonia
21	303	5.8	0.1	1,355	81	Ethiopia
–	–	1.1	1.3	33,159	84	Fiji
38	7,286	72.1	13.8	20,857	477	Finland
275	4,547	396.7	6.6	3,343	668	France
2	1,243	4.6	3.4	114,766	100	Gabon
–	–	0.3	0.2	5,019	22	Gambia
3	626	3.9	0.9	14,406	697	Georgia
348	4,218	856.6	10.0	1,862	571	Germany
8	386	6.9	0.3	2,314	48	Ghana
30	2,755	98.8	8.9	6,653	707	Greece
–	–	0.2	2.0	–	125	Grenada
8	616	11.2	0.9	8,410	166	Guatemala
–	–	1.5	0.2	23,042	182	Guinea
–	–	0.3	0.2	18,430	121	Guinea-Bissau
–	–	1.4	1.9	320,479	2,147	Guyana
–	–	1.7	0.2	1,599	119	Haiti
2	262	7.3	1.0	12,755	127	Honduras
4	548	58.9	5.8	10,353	770	Hungary
26	2,608	2.3	7.9	566,667	523	Iceland
3	11,976	1,199.0	1.0	1,670	615	India
573	531	368.0	1.7	12,441	381	Indonesia
174	800	407.6	6.1	1,931	1,071	Iran
146	2,166	84.4	3.3	2,490	1,742	Iraq
30	1,083	43.6	10.7	12,187	289	Ireland
15	3,738	63.8	9.4	240	324	Israel
21	3,049	482.2	8.0	3,289	772	Italy
184	3,171	10.9	4.1	3,520	156	Jamaica
4	1,541	1,304.2	10.0	3,351	694	Japan
533	4,173	19.4	3.6	148	191	Jordan
7	1,232	178.4	11.9	7,405	2,263	Kazakhstan
55	3,651	10.7	0.3	839	50	Kenya
17	506	0.0	0.3	–	–	Kiribati
–	–	73.1	3.3	3,403	400	Korea, North
20	910	507.0	11.0	1,448	392	Korea, South
213	4,431	70.5	28.6	7	184	Kuwait
25	10,212	6.0	1.2	3,821	1,989	Kyrgyzstan
3	546					

133

Countries	GDP Total US$ millions 2006 or latest available	Trade As % of GDP 2006		Investment Net inflow of FDI as % of GDP 2005	Aid Amount received as % of GDP 2005	Military expenditure 2006	
		goods	services			total	as % of GDP
Laos	3,437	61%	13%	1.0%	11.3%	13	0.4%
Latvia	20,116	87%	23%	4.6%	1.2%	279	1.4%
Lebanon	22,722	55%	86%	12.0%	1.2%	589	2.8%
Lesotho	1,494	149%	10%	6.3%	3.9%	33	2.3%
Liberia	631	107%	–	36.7%	56.8%	–	–
Libya	50,320	92%	7%		0.1%	593	1.1%
Lithuania	29,766	112%	21%	4.0%	1.2%	349	1.2%
Luxembourg	41,469	118%	198%	301.3%	–	254	0.6%
Macedonia	6,217	99%	17%	1.7%	4.0%	134	2.2%
Madagascar	5,499	40%	22%	0.6%	18.7%	298	5.2%
Malawi	3,164	73%	12%	0.1%	28.3%	20	0.9%
Malaysia	150,672	196%	32%	3.0%	0.0%	3,206	2.1%
Maldives	927	127%	67%	1.3%	9.2%	56	6.1%
Mali	5,866	50%	16%	3.0%	13.6%	132	2.2%
Malta	6,375	–	50%	–	0.1%	46	0.7%
Marshall Islands	155	92%	–	–	31.4%	–	–
Mauritania	2,663	74%	–	6.3%	10.0%	18	0.6%
Mauritius	6,347	90%	45%	0.6%	0.5%	18	0.3%
Mexico	839,182	62%	5%	2.4%	0.0%	3,229	0.4%
Micronesia, Fed. Sts.	245	65%	–	–	41.6%	–	–
Moldova	3,356	111%	30%	6.6%	5.6%	10	0.3%
Mongolia	3,132	112%	42%	8.7%	10.4%	19	0.8%
Montenegro*	2,491	99%	–	5.6%	4.4%	54	2.4%
Morocco	65,401	63%	23%	3.0%	1.3%	2,161	3.8%
Mozambique	6,833	71%	15%	1.6%	20.1%	57	0.8%
Namibia	6,566	86%	15%		2.0%	197	3.0%
Nepal	8,938	36%	11%	0.0%	5.7%	158	2.0%
Netherlands	662,296	134%	25%	6.5%	–	9,904	1.5%
New Zealand	104,519	47%	15%	1.8%	–	1,544	1.5%
Nicaragua	5,301	75%	15%	4.9%	15.4%	35	0.7%
Niger	3,663	38%	12%	0.4%	15.2%	38	1.1%
Nigeria	115,338	65%	12%	2.1%	7.6%	768	0.7%
Norway	334,942	60%	21%	1.1%	–	5,015	1.5%
Oman	30,835	–	14%	–	0.2%	3,276	9.0%
Pakistan	126,836	36%	10%	2.0%	1.5%	4,156	3.2%
Palestine Authority	4,059	–	–		25.0%	–	–
Panama	17,097	34%	33%	6.6%	0.1%	171	1.0%
Papua New Guinea	5,654	112%	30%	0.7%	5.8%	30	0.6%
Paraguay	9,275	88%	14%	0.9%	0.7%	67	0.7%
Peru	92,416	42%	6%	3.2%	0.5%	1,108	1.2%
Philippines	117,562	85%	10%	1.2%	0.5%	909	0.8%
Poland	338,733	69%	11%	3.2%	0.6%	6,235	1.8%
Portugal	194,726	57%	15%	1.7%	–	3,080	1.6%
Puerto Rico	–	–	–		–	–	–
Qatar	42,463	–	–	–	–	2,335	4.5%
Romania	121,609	69%	11%	6.7%	1.3%	2,324	1.9%
Russia	986,940	47%	8%	2.0%	0.2%	70,000	4.1%

* Data for Serbia and Montenegro that pre-date their separation in 2006 apply to the country as a single entity.

Economy and Environment

Energy Use Oil equivalent 2004		CO₂ Emissions Tonnes of CO₂ 2004		Water		Countries
total tonnes	kg per capita	total	per capita	Cubic metres of annual renewable water available per capita 2007	Cubic metres withdrawn per capita 2007	
–	–	1.4	0.2	53,859	541	Laos
5	1,988	7.1	3.1	15,521	125	Latvia
5	1,361	16.8	4.8	1,206	381	Lebanon
–	–	0.2	0.1	1,693	28	Lesotho
–	–	0.5	0.2	67,207	34	Liberia
18	3,169	49.8	8.7	99	883	Libya
9	2,666	13.0	3.8	7,317	78	Lithuania
5	10,481	11.7	25.8	6,499	108	Luxembourg
3	1,328	8.7	4.3	3,137	–	Macedonia
–	–	2.8	0.2	17,186	885	Madagascar
–	–	1.1	0.1	1,285	85	Malawi
57	2,279	149.2	6.0	22,104	376	Malaysia
–	–	0.7	2.3	87	17	Maldives
–	–	0.6	0.0	6,981	519	Mali
1	2,263	2.5	6.3	124	153	Malta
–	–	–	–	–	–	Marshall Islands
–	–	2.7	0.9	3,511	606	Mauritania
–	–	3.2	2.6	1,744	583	Mauritius
165	1,622	415.3	4.1	4,172	767	Mexico
–	–	–	–	–	–	Micronesia, Fed. Sts.
3	862	7.9	1.9	2,783	541	Moldova
–	–	8.6	3.4	12,837	172	Mongolia
–	56.7	7.0	–	19,870	–	Montenegro*
11	384	38.5	1.3	895	419	Morocco
9	441	2.0	0.1	10,531	35	Mozambique
1	665	2.7	1.3	8,658	153	Namibia
9	341	3.1	0.1	7,447	414	Nepal
82	5,045	187.1	11.5	5,539	494	Netherlands
18	4,344	33.1	8.1	79,893	549	New Zealand
3	643	4.4	0.9	34,416	244	Nicaragua
–	–	1.2	0.1	2,257	190	Niger
99	717	85.1	0.7	2,085	66	Nigeria
28	6,024	42.4	9.2	81,886	485	Norway
12	4,667	31.9	12.6	369	488	Oman
74	489	125.2	0.8	1,353	1,130	Pakistan
–	–	–	–	203	–	Palestine Authority
3	801	5.9	1.8	44,266	268	Panama
–	–	2.4	0.4	131,011	14	Papua New Guinea
4	694	4.1	0.7	52,133	85	Paraguay
13	479	29.6	1.1	66,431	752	Peru
44	542	80.3	1.0	5,577	363	Philippines
92	2,403	304.0	8.0	1,601	419	Poland
27	2,528	65.1	6.2	6,485	1,121	Portugal
–	–	–	–	1,776	–	Puerto Rico
18	23,246	39.1	50.3	62	483	Qatar
39	1,778	96.1	4.4	9,837	1,035	Romania
642	4,460	1,575.3	11.0	31,764	532	Russia

Countries	GDP Total US$ millions 2006 or latest available	Trade As % of GDP 2006		Investment Net inflow of FDI as % of GDP 2005	Aid Amount received as % of GDP 2005	Military expenditure 2006	
		goods	services			total	as % of GDP
Rwanda	2,494	25%	20%	0.4%	27.2%	72	2.4%
Samoa	424	55%	41%	–0.9%	11.5%	–	–
São Tomé and Principe	123	60%	–	6.2%	–	–	–
Saudi Arabia	349,138	–	11%	–	0.0%	29,514	8.5%
Senegal	9,186	56%	18%	0.7%	8.5%	149	1.6%
Serbia*	31,989	62%	–	5.6%	4.4%	812	2.5%
Seychelles	775	158%	86%	11.4%	2.8%	14	2.0%
Sierra Leone	1,450	42%	14%	4.8%	29.0%	24	1.7%
Singapore	132,158	386%	90%	17.2%	0.0%	6,321	4.8%
Slovakia	55,049	159%	20%	4.0%	0.6%	957	1.7%
Slovenia	37,303	127%	21%	1.6%	0.2%	629	1.7%
Solomon Islands	336	99%	–	–0.3%	66.5%	–	–
Somalia	–	–	–	–	–	–	–
South Africa	255,155	53%	10%	2.6%	0.3%	3,527	1.4%
Spain	1,224,676	43%	15%	2.0%	–	14,415	1.2%
Sri Lanka	26,964	63%	15%	1.2%	5.1%	943	3.4%
St. Kitts and Nevis	477	65%	52%	10.4%	0.9%	–	–
St. Lucia	899	73%	67%	13.1%	1.4%	–	–
St. Vincent and Grenadines	423	58%	56%	12.9%	1.2%	–	–
Sudan	37,442	34%	7%	8.3%	7.0%	524	1.5%
Suriname	2,115	131%	41%	–	3.8%	20	1.3%
Swaziland	2,648	162%	28%	–0.6%	1.7%	–	–
Sweden	383,799	71%	22%	3.0%	–	5,780	1.5%
Switzerland	380,412	76%	21%	4.2%	–	3,473	0.9%
Syria	33,407	53%	19%	1.5%	0.3%	1,739	5.1%
Tajikistan	2,811	110%	19%	2.4%	10.8%	73	2.7%
Tanzania	12,784	44%	19%	3.8%	12.2%	143	1.2%
Thailand	206,338	126%	27%	2.6%	–0.1%	2,275	1.1%
Togo	2,206	83%	19%	0.1%	4.1%	34	1.6%
Tonga	223	63%	–	2.1%	15.0%	–	–
Trinidad and Tobago	18,136	89%	10%	6.8%	0.0%	52	0.3%
Tunisia	30,298	87%	22%	2.5%	1.4%	435	1.4%
Turkey	402,710	55%	10%	2.7%	0.1%	11,630	2.9%
Turkmenistan	10,496	80%	–	0.8%	0.4%	184	1.8%
Uganda	9,419	39%	15%	2.9%	14.0%	192	1.9%
Ukraine	106,469	79%	20%	9.1%	0.5%	1,723	1.6%
United Arab Emirates	129,702	–	–	–	0.0%	9,482	6.7%
United Kingdom	2,376,984	45%	17%	7.2%	–	55,444	2.3%
United States	13,163,870	22%	6%	0.9%	–	535,943	4.0%
Uruguay	19,308	46%	11%	4.3%	0.1%	227	1.2%
Uzbekistan	17,178	54%	–	0.3%	1.2%	85	0.5%
Vanuatu	388	50%	49%	3.6%	11.5%	–	–
Venezuela	181,862	51%	4%	2.0%	0.0%	2,588	1.4%
Vietnam	60,999	138%	18%	3.7%	3.7%	3,439	5.6%
Yemen	19,057	73%	9%	–1.6%	2.2%	824	4.2%
Zambia	10,734	61%	14%	3.6%	13.9%	245	2.4%
Zimbabwe	–	80%	–	3.0%	11.4%	156	2.8%

* Data for Serbia and Montenegro that pre-date their separation in 2006 apply to the country as a single entity.

Economy and Environment

Energy Use Oil equivalent 2004		CO₂ Emissions Tonnes of CO₂ 2004		Water		Countries
total tonnes	kg per capita	total	per capita	Cubic metres of annual renewable water available per capita 2007	Cubic metres withdrawn per capita 2007	
–	–	0.6	0.1	551	18	Rwanda
–	–	0.2	0.8	–	–	Samoa
–	–	0.1	0.6	13,293	51	São Tomé and Principe
140	6,232	342.9	15.2	93	736	Saudi Arabia
3	242	5.1	0.4	3,225	225	Senegal
–	–	56.7	7.0	19,870	–	Serbia*
–	–	0.5	6.5	–	150	Seychelles
–	–	1.1	0.2	27,577	80	Sierra Leone
26	6,034	50.1	11.8	135	82	Singapore
18	3,407	39.8	7.4	9,276	–	Slovakia
7	3,591	16.3	8.2	16,219	–	Slovenia
–	–	0.2	0.4	89,044	–	Solomon Islands
–	–	–	–	1,620	307	Somalia
131	2,829	427.9	9.2	1,048	279	South Africa
142	3,331	355.1	8.3	2,557	870	Spain
9	485	13.1	0.7	2,372	666	Sri Lanka
–	–	0.1	2.7	546	–	St. Kitts and Nevis
–	–	0.4	2.3	–	109	St. Lucia
–	–	0.2	1.7	–	86	St. Vincent and Grenadines
18	497	10.8	0.3	1,707	1,135	Sudan
–	–	2.3	5.2	268,132	1,551	Suriname
–	–	1.0	0.9	4,400	975	Swaziland
54	5,998	56.1	6.2	19,131	335	Sweden
27	3,672	44.6	6.0	7,354	358	Switzerland
18	993	51.7	2.8	1,314	1,148	Syria
3	516	5.5	0.9	2,392	1,931	Tajikistan
19	500	4.5	0.1	2,291	143	Tanzania
97	1,524	238.5	3.7	6,280	1,400	Thailand
3	449	2.3	0.4	2,272	35	Togo
–	–	0.1	1.1	–	–	Tonga
11	8,675	21.8	16.8	2,925	239	Trinidad and Tobago
9	876	23.8	2.4	442	271	Tunisia
82	1,151	229.2	3.2	3,051	534	Turkey
16	3,265	39.5	8.3	4,979	5,140	Turkmenistan
–	–	2.1	0.1	2,133	12	Uganda
140	2,958	329.6	6.9	3,066	767	Ukraine
44	10,142	104.0	24.1	31	787	United Arab Emirates
234	3,906	551.3	9.0	2,449	161	United Kingdom
2,326	7,920	5,888.7	20.0	6,816	1,647	United States
3	867	6.0	1.7	39,612	929	Uruguay
54	2,088	131.9	5.1	1,842	2,269	Uzbekistan
–	–	0.1	0.4	–	–	Vanuatu
56	2,149	140.2	5.4	44,545	332	Venezuela
50	612	91.8	1.1	10,310	889	Vietnam
6	313	19.2	0.9	184	343	Yemen
7	605	2.4	0.2	8,726	163	Zambia
9	719	10.0	0.8	1,520	328	Zimbabwe

Sources

For sources available on the internet, in most cases only the root address has been given. To view the source, it is recommended that the reader type the title of the page or document into Google or another search engine.

Introduction
Dependent population
UN Population Division. World Population Prospects. The 2006 Revision. http://esa.un.org/unpp
Causes of death
WHO. World Health Report 2004. www.who.int
Energy production
International Energy Agency: World Energy Statistics 2007. www.iea.org

Part One: Who We Are
18–19 Population
People in the world
Population cartogram created by: ODT, Inc. www.odtmaps.com using data from US State Department.

Annual percentage change: WDI online database.
Population growth
CIA Factbook. www.cia.gov

20–21 Life Expectancy
Life expectancy
Changing expectancy
Health and wealth
World average life expectancy
World Bank estimates from sources including census reports, UN Population Division's World Population Prospects, national statistic offices, household surveys conducted by national agencies, and Macro International. Downloaded from WDI online. Data for Afghanistan and Iraq from: State of the world's children. 2007. New York: UNICEF 2006.
GNI in purchasing power parity dollars from WDI Online.
The average lifespan...
Kinsella KG. Changes in life expectancy 1900–1990. The American Journal of Clinical Nutrition.1992;55:1196S-1202S. www.ajcn.org

22–23 Ethnicity and Diversity
Turner B. The statesman's yearbook 2008: the politics, cultures and economies of the world. London: Palgrave Macmillan; 2007.
MSN Encarta encyclopaedia. http://encarta.msn.com
US Central Intelligence Agency. The world factbook. www.cia.gov
Refugees International. www.refugeesinternational.org

24–25 Religious Beliefs
O'Brien J, Palmer M. The atlas of religion. London: Earthscan. Berkeley and Los Angeles: University of California Press; 2007
CIA. The World Factbook

26–27 Education
Primary education
Secondary education
Tertiary education
United Nations Educational, Scientific, and Cultural Organization (UNESCO) Institute for Statistics. Downloaded from World Development Indicators online database.
Adult literacy
Bangladesh and India
UNDP. Human Development Report 2007/08. Table 1.
Sub-Saharan Africa
57% of children...
UNDP. Human Development Report 2007/08. Table 30.

28–29 Urbanization
UN World Urbanization Prospects. Downloaded from WDI online.
50% of people...
State of the world's cities 2006/7. London: Earthscan for UN-Habitat; 2006.

30–31 Diversity of Cities
Global Cities: Exhibition at Tate Modern, London, June–August 2007 www.tate.org.uk
City Mayors Statistics www.citymayors.com
State of the world's cities 2006/7. London: Earthscan for UN-Habitat; 2006.
Encarta online encyclopaedia: http://encarta.msn.com

32–33 Global Movement
UN Department of Economic and Social Affairs. Population Division. International Migration 2006.

Part Two: Wealth and Power
36–37 Gross National Income
All data downloaded from WDI online database.

38–39 Inequality
Distribution of wealth
Gini index: WDI online.
Unemployment: Human Development Report 2007/2008. Fighting climate change: Human solidarity in a divided world. New York: UNDP; 2007. Table 21.
Russia – New York Times. 2007 Nov 29, quoting Forbes Rich List and World Bank.
South Africa – Merill Lynch/Capgemini 11th World Wealth Report, quoted in: South Africa the Good News. 2 July 2007 July 2. www.sagoodnews.co.za
USA – Forbes Rich List 2008 and calculation based on Human Development Report 2007/2008. New York: UNDP; 2007. Table 4: Human and income poverty.
Poor people in rich countries
Human Development Report 2007/2008. Table 4.
In the hands of the few
Forbes Rich List 2008 www.forbes.com
The wealth of the 100 richest people...
www.forbes.com
World Bank.

40–41 Quality of Life
Relative human development
UNDP. Human development report 2007–08. Fighting climate change: Human solidarity in a divided world. New York: UNDP; 2007. Table 1: Human development index.
Healthy water
UNDP. Human Development Report 2006. Beyond scarcity: Power, poverty and the global water crisis. New York: UNDP; 2006.
Poor sanitation...
State of the world's cities 2006/7. London: Earthscan for UN-Habitat; 2006.

42–43 Transnationals
Corporate wealth
GNI (current US$) 2006 from WDI online database.
Forbes 2000 largest companies by assets. 2007 March. www.forbes.com/lists.
The global mix
United Nations Conference on Trade and Development (UNCTAD). World investment report 2007, Annex table A.I.5.
1.8 million people...
UNCTAD. World investment report 2007, Annex Table A.I.13.
Global players
UNCTAD. World investment report 2007. Annex A, Table A.I.16 and A.I.15. The top 100 TNCs and non-TNCs by the number of host countries.

44–45 Foreign Investment
Elliott, L. Oil money is coming – and there is little the West can do about it. The Guardian. 2008 March 1:40-41.
Importance of inward investment
WDI online.

Attractiveness to investors
United Nations Conference on Trade and Development (UNCTAD). Inward FDI Indices. www.unctad.org

46–47 Trade
Importance of trade
World Trade Organization and World Bank GDP estimates.
Merchandise exports
Changing places
WTO. International Trade Statistics 2008. Table II.2. World merchandise exports by major product group and region, 2006. www.wto.org
World trade in merchandise grew...
WTO 2008 op.cit. Table 1.6.

48–49 Communications
OECD Factbook 2007. Telephone access.
Telephones
In Africa
International Telecommunications Union (ITU) via WDI online.
OECD Factbook 2007. Telephone access.
Where the money is made
OECD. Communications Outlook 2007.
Internet access
International Telecommunications Union (ITU). Accessed via WDI online database.
Most popular internet search engines
Searchers
comScore via BBC News. Google dominates world search. 2007 October 11. http://news.bbc.co.uk
Mobiles in Africa
International Telecommunications Union (ITU).

50–51 Energy Trade
IEA. World Energy Outlook 2007. Executive Summary. www.iea.org
Who holds the power?
International Energy Agency and United Nations, Energy statistics yearbook. Downloaded from WDI online.
USA – US Department of Energy. Biomass. FAQs. www1.eere.energy.gov
Germany, Ukraine – BBC. Russian gas cut will not hit EU. 2005 Dec 30. http://news.bbc.co.uk
Russia – BBC. Russia plants flag under North Pole. 2007 Aug 2. http://news.bbc.co.uk
BBC. Russia ahead in Arctic gold rush. 2007 Aug 1. http://news.bbc.co.uk
Japan – International Energy Agency and United Nations, Energy statistics yearbook.
China – China Institute, University of Alberta. China's crude oil imports up 12.3 pct in 2007. www.uofaweb.ualberta.ca

52–53 Tourism
World Tourism Organization. Yearbook of tourism statistics, compendium of tourism statistics and data files, and IMF and World Bank exports estimates.

54–55 Debt and Aid
Aid received
Debt servicing costs
Development Assistance Committee of the Organisation for Economic Co-operation and Development, and World Bank GNI estimates. Downloaded from WDI online.
Official development assistance
Falling short
HDR 2007/08 Table 17 OECD-DAC country expenditures on aid
Only 3% of money...
www.aafrc.org
NCVO, CAF. Results of the 2006/07 Individual Giving Survey on charitable giving with special reports on gender and causes. www.ncvo-vol.org.uk

Part Three: War and Peace
58–59 War in the 21st Century
Smith D. The atlas of war & peace. New York: Penguin and London: Earthscan; 2003.
Uppsala University, Uppsala Conflict Data Program. www.pcr.uu.se

60–61 Warlords and Militias
Non-state wars
Number of non-state wars
Uppsala University, Uppsala Conflict Data Program. www.pcr.uu.se Press reports.
Child soldiers
Coalition to Stop the Use of Child Soldiers. Global report 2004. 222.child-soldiers.org, cited in The World Bank and Human Security Report Project. Miniatlas of human security. 2008.
Campaigns of violence against civilian populations
Uppsala Conflict Data Program, Uppsala University/Human Security Report Projects dataset, 2006.

62–63 Terrorism
BBC world news http://news.bbc.co.uk
Country reports by International Crisis Group. www.crisisgroup.org
Press reports.

64–65 Military Spending
Military spending
Total military spending
International Institute for Strategic Studies (IISS). The military balance 2008. London: Routledge; 2008. Table 37.
Arms transfer agreements
Grimmett RF. Conventional arms transfers to developing nations 1999–2006. Figure 1. Washington DC: Congressional Research Service http://opencrs.com/document/RL34187.
Recipients of arms transfers
Grimmett RF. op. cit. Tables 1C and 1E.

66–67 Armed Forces
Armed forces
International Institute for Strategic Studies (IISS). The military balance 2008. London: Routledge; 2008. Table 37.
Conscription
The military balance 2008.
US Central Intelligence Agency. The World Factbook. www.cia.gov
Total number of active military personnel...
The military balance 2008. Table 37.
Warlords and militias
The military balance 2008. Table 47.

68–69 Peacekeeping
UN Peacekeeping. www.un.org/Depts/dpko/dpko
Department of Political Affairs. www0.un.org/Depts/dpa/fieldmissions.html
IISS. The military balance 2008. London: IISS; 2008.

70–71 Casualties of War
Battle deaths since World War II
Battle deaths in the 21st century
UCDP/PRIO Armed Conflict dataset v.4-2007, 1946–2006. www.prio.no
Deaths in Iraq
Iraq Body Count. www.iraqbodycount.net/database
Iraq Coalition Casualties. www.icasualties.org
Burnham G, Lafta R, Doocy S, Roberts L. Mortality after the 2003 invasion of Iraq: a cross-sectional cluster sample survey. The Lancet; 2006 October 11.
Iraqi health minister estimates as many as 150,000 Iraqis killed by insurgents. International Herald Tribune. 2006 November 9.
Iraq poll 2007: in graphics. BBC News. 2007 March 19. http://news.bbc.co.uk
More than 1,000,000 Iraqis murdered. 2007 September. Opinion Research Business. www.opinion.co.uk
Update on Iraqi Casualty Data. Opinion Research Business, 2008 January. www.opinion.co.uk
The deadliest conflicts
Death tolls for the major wars and atrocities of the twentieth century. http://users.erols.com/mwhite28/warstat2.htm
Persistent killers
International Campaign to Ban Landmines. Landmine monitor report 2007: toward a mine-free world. www.icbl.org

72–73 Refugees
United Nations High Commissioner for Refugees. UNHCR statistical yearbook 2006. www.unhcr.org/statistics.html

United Nations Relief and Works Agency for Palestinian Refugees in the Near East. Map of UNRWA's Area of Operations. www.un.org/unrwa/refugees/images/map.jpg

US Committee for Refugees and Immigrants. World refugee survey 2007. www.refugees.org

74–75 Global Peace
Vision of Humanity: Global Peace Index. www.visionofhumanity.org

Part Four: Rights and Respect

78–79 Political Systems
Political systems
Country reports of the International Crisis Group, Brussels. www.icg.org

Human Development Report 2007/2008. New York: United Nations Development Programme; 2007.

BBC News http://news.bbc.co.uk/1/hi/world

Voter turnout
International Idea. www.idea.int

80–81 Religious Freedom
O'Brien J, Palmer M. The atlas of religion. London: Earthscan, Los Angeles and Berkeley: University of California Press; 2007.

82–83 Press Freedom
Freedom of the press
Press freedom
Only 18%...
Freedom House. Freedom of the press 2008. www.freedomhouse.org

Journalists murdered
International Federation of Journalists. Journalists put to the sword in 2006. IFJ 2007. www.ifj.org

84–85 Human Rights Abuses
Extreme abuse of human rights
Amnesty International report 2008: The state of the world's human rights. London: Amnesty International; 2008.

Amnesty International. "Rendition" and secret detention: A global system of human rights violations. Questions and answers. London: Amnesty International; 2006.

Human Rights Watch country reports www.hrw.org

Human Rights Watch World Report 2007 www.hrw.org

Extraordinary rendition
Council of Europe, Alleged secret detentions and unlawful inter-state transfers of detainees involving Council of Europe member states; Report by the Committee on Legal Affairs and Human Rights (Rapporteur: Mr Dick Marty). Doc. 10957. 2006 June 12. www.coe.int

Secret detentions and illegal transfers of detainees involving Council of Europe member states; Second report by the Committee on Legal Affairs and Human Rights (Rapporteur: Mr Dick Marty), Doc. 11302. rev, 2007 June 11. www.coe.int

2001–08 Guantanamo
GlobalSecurity.org 2008 May 02.

Executions
Death sentences and executions in 2007. AI Index: ACT 50/001/2008. London: Amnesty International Secretariat; 2008 April 15.

Judicial killings
Amnesty International USA, 1 January 2007. www.amnestyusa.org World moves closer to abolition of the death penalty. Amnesty International USA. www.amnestyusa.org

Death penalty laws in your state. www.amnestyusa.org

86–87 Trafficking and Sex Tourism
Trafficking
Trafficking exists...
Child trafficking in Europe: a broad vision to put children first. United Nations Children's Fund Innocenti Research Centre; 2008. www.unicef-irc.org

Trafficking in human beings, especially women and children, in Africa. United Nations Children's Fund Innocenti Research Centre: 2005. www.unicef-irc.org

Travelling Sex Offenders
Legislation
Draft working paper on the prevention of sexual exploitation of children in travel and tourism. United Nations Children's Fund

Innocenti Research Centre; Forthcoming publication 2008.

Some countries are mainly reported to be origin of travelling sex offenders, while others are mainly reported as destinations. Some countries may be origin and destination at the same time. For others, information is not yet available.

Caribbean trafficking routes
Guatemala
Mexico
In modern bondage: sex trafficking in the Americas. International Human Rights Law Institute, DePaul University College of Law. 2002 October.

Australia, Japan, New Zealand – Prostitution of children and child-sex tourism. an analysis of domestic and international responses. National Centre for Missing and Exploited Children; 1999.

Eastern Europe, Men known as "lover boys"...
Child trafficking in Europe. op. cit.

Brazil –Mattar MY. The role of the government in combating trafficking in persons - a global human rights approach; 2003 October 29. www.protectionproject.org/commentary/ctp.htm

Cambodia, Thailand – Regional consultation for Asia and the Pacific on the protection of children from sexual exploitation in tourism. World Tourism Organization (UNWTO); 2003:82.

Canada – Global Monitoring Report on the status of action against commercial sexual exploitation of children. ECPAT; 2006:11.

Lithuania – Looking back, thinking forward: the fourth report on the implementation of the agenda for action adopted at the First World Congress against Commercial Sexual Exploitation of Children. Stockholm, Sweden, 1996. Stockholm: Swedish International Development Agency; 1999-2000.

UK – Sexual Offences Act 2003. Chapter 42, Section 114

Over 1.2 million children...
ILO: A Future Without Child Labour; 2002.

88–89 Children's Rights
Birth registration
UNICEF Statistics. Birth Registration. www.childinfo.org
Children not in school
Where children are working
Although the number...
Hagemann F, Diallo Y, Etienne A, Mehran F. Global child labour trends 2000 to 2004. ILO; 2006. www.ilo.org

See also: www.ilo.org/ipec/index.htm

90–91 Women's Rights
Equal rights
UNDP. Human development report 2007/2008. Fighting climate change: human solidarity in a divided world. New York: UNDP; 2007.

National parliament
UN Women's Indicators and Statistics Database, downloaded from WDI online.

Only 35 countries have...
Seager J. The atlas of women. Berkeley: University of California Press and London: Earthscan; 2009.

In Norway it is a legal requirement...
Fouche G, Treanor J. In Norway, a woman's place is in the boardroom. 2006 January 9. www.guardian.co.uk

Women earners
HDR 2007/2008. Table 31. Gender inequality in economic activity.

92–93 Gay Rights
Legislation on homosexuality
The Guardian 2007 April 14. pp.20–21, based on: Ottosson D. State-sponsored homophobia. A world survey of laws prohibiting same-sex activity between consenting adults. ILGA; 2007. www.ilga.org Cross-checked and updated against:

Johnson R. Where is gay life legal? http://gaylife.about.com

Grossman CL. Gay civil union not as divisive as marriage. www.usatoday.com

LGBT adoption. en.wikipedia.org/wiki/LGBT_adoption

Part Five Health of the People

96–97 Malnutrition
WHO. Micronutrient deficiencies. www.who.int